A Guide to

Modern

Freemasonry

Also by Robert E. Burtt

A Pennsylvania Masonic Handbook:
The Personal Ahiman Rezon

Rome: A Commonplace Book

Wait Until Sunset: Memories of a Distant Conflict

Heart of the Mystery: A Novel

A
Guide to
Modern
Freemasonry

By

Robert E. Burtt

Creare Spazio Editrice

Burtt, Robert E.

A Guide to Modern Freemasonry

Includes bibliographical references

ISBN-10: 1482788314
ISBN-13: 978-1482788310

Manufactured in the United States of America

Creare Spazio Editrice

by

Createspace, a division of Amazon
7290 Investment Drive, Suite B
North Charleston, SC 29418

2nd Edition, 2021

Dedicated to the memory of
Brother James F. Standish, P.M.
1937-2012

Brother James was a dedicated Freemason, husband, father, grandfather, and health care executive. Past Master of George Bartram-Paul Sands Lodge 298, Springfield PA. He was a member of Chester Royal Arch Chapter No. 258, Riblah Council No. 59, Royal and Select Master Masons, and the Scottish Rite Bodies of the Valley of Philadelphia. He also served on the Committee of the Academy of Masonic Knowledge, and was Secretary of the Pennsylvania Lodge of Research. A past member of the Board of Directors for the Masonic Home of Pennsylvania, he was an active force on the Grand Lodge of Pennsylvania's Committee on Masonic Homes.   A committed Presbyterian, Bro. James's faith served to illuminate his life. He was the first Masonic scholar to encourage the author in his writing career. We are confident that Jim has taken his station or place in the celestial lodge above, "that house not made with hands, eternal in the heavens!"

There are few written works that are the exclusive product of a single mind. This book is no different. The author would particularly like to thank the following persons who, directly or indirectly, helped to inspire this project.

Bro. Ed King, Grand Lodge of Maine
Bro. Jim Knights, Harmony Lodge No. 429, GL of PA
Ms. Carole Alfe, Manager, Museum Shop
& Ms. Cathy Giaimo, Asst. Librarian,
both of
The Masonic Library & Museum of the
Grand Lodge of Pennsylvania
Dr. Jeffrey Wolfe

Finally, I must include a special acknowledgement. Without the love and support of my wife Grace, I would never have been able to type a word. All of my achievements—such as they are—are just as much hers as mine.

"We met upon the Level.

And we're parting on the Square."

--Traditional Masonic farewell

*"Behold, how good and how pleasant it is for
Brethren to dwell together in unity!"*

Psalms 133:1.

TABLE OF CONTENTS

Tile

     To "Tile" means to post a guard at the entrance of a Masonic lodge room in order to keep out non-Masons and other unauthorized people. This sentinel is called the "Tiler." The word is sometimes spelled "Tyler." The origin of the term is obscure. It first appeared in print in 1738. The most common explanation among Masonic scholars is that early stone masons were responsible for completing the roof of the structures they built. Many roofs were constructed of tiles. Therefore, the person who was responsible for concealing, covering, and protecting the lodge room was given the name of the "Tiler."
All Masonic meetings open with a ceremony in which the lodge's outer doors are locked and guarded. This procedure is called "Tiling the lodge."* Even to this day, the Tiler is armed with a ceremonial sword (similar to the one above).

It is a fact that Freemason wear aprons during their meetings. Aprons were worn by workmen, in the building trades especially, throughout history. This is a fair representation of a Masonic one. In color it is white, with light blue trim. All decorations or lettering are also of sky blue. Usually made of cloth but often of leather or actual lambskin. Normal size is 18 by 18 inches. It is the "mark of a Freemason and symbolic of the highest honor that a Brother can attain. It is meant to remind the Freemason that his personal conduct should be clean and spotless and that he should strive to emulate the innocence of the lamb. Note the flap at the top, often adorned with the number of the lodge. The author's Masonic home is Harmony Lodge Number 429, Zelienople, Pennsylvania, in the United States.

INTRODUCTION:
"Why another Masonic Book?"

Anyone who feels the need to write a book on the subject of Freemasonry needs to explain himself very, very, thoroughly. Freemasonry is one of those areas that could be said to suffer from literary overkill. Ever since the Fraternity made its modern public appearance in 1717, printing presses have produced a torrent of writings dealing with every imaginable aspect of this group. Today, one has only to initiate a quick internet search to find enough material to sate any curious impulse. Why would anyone think that another Masonic book is needed?

The current state of affairs illustrates my excuse, if you will, for writing this short work. There is too *much* information about Freemasonry in print. There are too many wild theories about the group. Conspiracy peddlers have made careers out of lurid speculation. There is way too much "noise" in the public square about Freemasons. Where can one turn for a quick, trustworthy overview? How is one to pick from the thousands of titles available?

Freemasonry has become a staple of cable television. Religious, historical, and documentary channels all seem to see Masonry as a sure-fire programing ploy to gain market share. All of this overload just makes a confusing and complex subject even more perplexing for the interested layman. What is needed is a short, easily understood overview of the fascinating world of the Freemasons.

I did not set out to solve this problem. A few years ago, I wrote a minor Masonic work dealing with a very limited topic: Freemasonry in Pennsylvania. Although by no means a best-seller, it has enjoyed some small success. Soon friends, interested readers, and booksellers started asking me for another book. I was unprepared for such a response. I had moved on to other writing projects and was loath to backtrack into an area that I felt I had already covered. It took some time before I could prepare myself to tackle the subject again.

What ultimately convinced me was a plea from a friend who ran the gift shop located within the Grand Lodge of Pennsylvania in Philadelphia. The structure is listed in the National Register of Historic Landmarks and is one of the city's more interesting tourist attractions.* Visitors often end their day by stopping to buy souvenirs and reading material. Most are members of the general public and know little or nothing about Freemasonry. Often they ask for a "good book" about the Fraternity. When they are shown the selection, many assume a panic-stricken look and ask something along the lines of "don't you have anything smaller? I don't want to become an expert. Isn't 350 pages a little long?"

It is my belief that many casual laypersons who wish to learn a little about Freemasonry want just that: to learn a *little* about the Craft. They don't want to embark upon an extensive investigation involving several books and thousands of pages. They simply want a quick overview of the Fraternity and maybe get the answers to a few basic questions. After satisfying their curiosity, they wish to move on.

It is with this audience in mind that I have decided to pen this little work. I make no pretensions to original scholarship. I have done more than a little Masonic research in my life and hopefully this will illuminate my writing. The title, however, is meant to be literal. This is simply a guide—an overview—of a complex phenomenon.

I *can* claim some expertise as an active participant in Freemasonry. In the interest of full disclosure to the reader, I must admit to have been deeply involved in Freemasonry for almost twenty years. I have held most of the offices within my Masonic lodge, and served as Worshipful Master (President) during 2001. I have also been active in many of the ancillary bodies of the Craft.

I have been the head of a Royal Arch Chapter, a leader of a Council of Royal and Select Master Masons, and was the principal officer of a Commandery of Knights Templar. I received the 32nd Degree in the Scottish Rite branch of Freemasonry, and was a "Shriner" at my local Temple. I have held educational positions within my local Masonic District, and am a charter member of the Pennsylvania Lodge of Research.

Although impressive-sounding, this list of offices and titles simply means that I was a very active member of the Craft. I was a leader at the local level, but unfortunately moved away from my home state before I got any higher. In the last few years, my Masonic career has taken a more quiet turn. I feel that I can best contribute to the Fraternity by explaining it to a larger, wider audience through my writing.

Freemasonry as a subject for study seems to be an endless source of fascination to a sizable portion of the reading public. Its traditions, rites, customs, dress, and history form a long and storied tale. It is one of only three truly international organizations with world-wide goals. The Roman Catholic Church and the United Nations are also devoted to spreading their individual visions of peace and unity to the entire world. Freemasonry is dedicated to exemplifying a *religiously neutral* philosophy of "The Brotherhood of Man under the Fatherhood of God." Since its inception in the early 18th Century, Freemasonry has spread to most of the countries of the world.

This book will try to cover the most common areas

of public curiosity. We will start with the psychological basis of the Fraternity and its methods of education. Next, we will move on to an examination of some of the various symbols used. A short overview of the history of the Fraternity will be explored as well as the state of Masonry today—in the early Twenty-First Century.

The ceremonies of the organization will be covered next, although with one important caveat. As an active member, I have promised not to reveal certain aspects of our rituals, so the reader will not receive every last bit of information. I promise you however (being a man of my word), that what is left out of this volume will be of negligible value. To quote Brother Benjamin Franklin: "The Great Secret of Freemasonry is that there is no Secret at all!"*

An actual Masonic meeting will be detailed and explained. The most common question that I get from friends, relatives, and co-workers is: "what do you guys actually *do* at your meetings?" I will try to do my level best (a Masonic expression now in common usage) to show what it's like to be a member.

One of the confusing aspects of the Masonic world is the variety of groups and bodies that compose it. To the outsider, Freemasonry is a kaleidoscope of aprons, gloves, swords, fezzes, jewels, necklaces, hats, turbans, and cloaks. It is a complex system, but it can be simplified. I will attempt to do so for the reader.

Once the history of the Order has been covered, the health of the movement at the present time and its future will be addressed. Without spoiling anything, I will admit that the future does not look bright for Freemasonry. Much of the Twentieth Century looked like a triumphal march for the Brotherhood. In the year 1960, it looked to some as if Freemasonry's hold on Western society was assured, and its future path one of growth and unlimited expansion. This is no longer the case, both in the United States, as well as overseas. There are a few bright spots, but not many, as we shall see.

Finally, we will close this book with a meditation on the ultimate purpose of Freemasonry and its value, both to the individual, and to society as a whole. In closing, other books and areas of research will be recommended for the casual reader who might want to explore "The Brotherhood" further.

Despite recent popular depictions, Freemasonry is not a totally solemn, humorless organization. Role-play, acting, jokes, extemporaneous speaking, and amateur dramatics are integral parts of the experience. I hope to reveal this side of Masonry. Sprinkled throughout this work are symbols, drawings, and signs that will gradually illuminate the workings of the Order. I do not recommend skipping chapters or flitting from page to page at random. My design is to build gradually with good materials so that the edifice, once erected, will stand the test of time. (This manner of speaking is a good example of Masonic expression). I hope, dear reader, that you enjoy my efforts.

The "All-Seeing Eye," an important Masonic symbol. It represents the omnipresence and watchfulness of the Supreme Being (or God). "The eyes of the Lord are in every place, keeping watch on the evil and the good." (Proverbs 15:3). It serves to remind Freemasons that we will be answerable for our actions in this life. *

Fanciful depiction of the entrance to the Temple of King
Solomon at Jerusalem. Temple imagery figures largely in Freemasonry.

Opening

All meetings of a formal nature have some sort of procedure for starting. Masonic lodge meetings employ a formal ceremony, called the "Opening," that can last for some time. There are several steps in this process. First, it must be ascertained if all present are dressed properly, that is in dress clothes and wearing a Masonic Apron. Then, the members must be assured that there are no "outsiders," or non-Freemasons present. Next, the doors to the lodge room are secured and locked. A formal explanation of the duties of lodge officers is recited, and the Worshipful Master (presiding officer) of the lodge admonishes all those present to embrace peace and harmony during the meeting. Next, an invocation is recited invoking the blessing of God on all present. Finally, the lodge meeting is declared open.* In order for a lodge to be officially ready to do business, a Bible must be opened in the center of the room, with a square and compasses on top of it. The reason for this will be explained later in this book.

Some Famous Freemasons

Astronaut Edwin "Buzz" Aldrin, Gene Autry, Sen. Howard Baker, Irving Berlin, Simon Bolivar, Actor Ernest Bourgnine, James Boswell, Luther Burbank, Winston Churchill, Henry Clay, "Buffalo Bill" Cody, George M. Cohan, Cecil B. De Mille, Gen. James Doolittle, Sir Arthur Conan Doyle, "Duke" Ellington, W.C. Fields, Henry Ford, Benjamin Franklin, Giuseppe Garibaldi, Edward Gibbon, J.W. Goethe, "Gus" Grissom, John Hancock, Franz Haydn, J. Edgar Hoover, Rogers Hornsby, Harry Houdini, Sam Houston, John Paul Jones, Rudyard Kipling, Marquis de Lafayette, Charles Lindbergh, Gen. Douglas Mac Arthur, George C. Marshall, Chief Justice John Marshall, Justice Thurgood Marshall, Christy Mathewson, W. A. Mozart, Gen. John Pershing, Paul Revere, Eddie Rickenbacker, Will Rogers, Sir Walter Scott, "Red" Skelton, John Philip Sousa, Harry Truman, Mark Twain, Voltaire, Chief Justice Earl Warren, Booker T. Washington, Pres. George Washington, John Wayne.*

PSYCHOLOGY OF THE FRATERNITY

I can almost hear you asking: "what in the world does psychology have to do with Freemasonry? When are we going to get to the 'good stuff:' the crazy ceremonies, the costumes, and the weird things those old guys do? If the pace of this book doesn't 'pick up' soon, I'm dropping it!" Bear with me for a while dear reader. I promise that all of that "good stuff" will be covered in due time. We must first begin at a basic level and ask fundamental questions.

One of the curious things about the organization has been its staying power, and its enduring fascination and attraction to its members. Ever wonder why? In other words, what is Freemasonry *grounded* on? Why does it still exist? My answer to this query is that the foundation of the Order is partly to be found in the human makeup, particularly the mind.

When examining any phenomenon, a real danger is going back to first principles until one arrives at the story of Adam. I won't go that far, but we must begin with one of the foundations of the modern world: the Eighteenth Century movement known as "The Enlightenment."

The Enlightenment was a complex period in European history that expressed itself in a variety of ways according to national character. The movement was very different in Scotland than it was in France, for example. Rousseau and Adam Smith were unalike in temperament, lifestyle, and interests. While very difficult to summarize, there are several discrete elements within it.

The Enlightenment immediately followed the rise of the modern scientific method in the late Seventeenth Century. Newton, Descartes, and Leibniz are generally considered the leading minds of this period. The invention of modern science was an important precursor for what was to follow. Enlightenment thought was generally hostile to superstition, skeptical of established authority, especially in matters of religion and politics, and open to reason and rationality as the governing norm for society.*

Thinkers like Montesquieu, Kant, and Thomas Paine saw prejudice, intolerance, and superstition as major causes of evil amongst the human race. They saw humans as "perfectible." If educational standards were raised, and the natural tendencies of human intelligence allowed free play, then society would improve, political understanding would increase, and the civilization would advance.

The Enlightenment movement tried to encourage open-mindedness, freedom of thought and expression, as well as individual rights and liberty. The American and French Revolutions were the ultimate examples of these ideals translated into action. During the Eighteenth Century the educated population of Europe became more and more enthralled with this new vision of humanity. In every country they tended to gather together to share information, debate new ideas, and keep in touch with other like-minded individuals.

In each nation these groups met in differing venues. Englishmen embraced the institution of the "Coffee House," where newspapers were readily available, intellectuals debated new ideas, and an exciting new beverage fueled middle-class progressive dreams. In France, the *Salon* became an institution where, usually under the sponsorship of noble *Grande dames*,* thinkers like Voltaire and Rousseau exposed the shortcomings of the French monarchy. In Germany and Austria, Academies were formed where social improvements and ideas for bettering the individual and the state were explored.

At the center of this continent-wide movement was Freemasonry. The Brotherhood made its appearance in London in 1717 and quickly spread to every nation in Europe. Much of its appeal finds echoes in modern examinations of the Craft. It was an organization dedicated to helping its members achieve a higher level of moral and spiritual development. Lodges were also organized—partly by accident—as "laboratories of republicanism."

Each lodge, although part of a larger, national organization, was set up as a self-governing body. Officers were elected by the membership for specific, set terms. Each lodge had a constitution—a set of rules which all members and officers promised to abide by. Finally, each Freemason had been elected by the other members and entered into fellowship with his "brethren" on equal terms, with equal rights and obligations. These obligations extended to himself, his brothers, his lodge, and to Freemasonry in general.

In the early 1700's this mindset was revolutionary. Monarchies rightly feared that Masonic lodges could become cradles for massive social change. In France, the Parisian police became worried about such republican activities and their ultimate effect on social order.*

In a work this short, simplification is perhaps a necessity. Broad brush strokes are required, else this book would become an uncontrollable monster. Although we have ignored the subtleties of Enlightenment Thought, hopefully the "spirit of the age" has come through.

Individual man was seen as a perfectible creature, with untapped resources in his intellect. In one of Locke's easily misunderstood passages, the human mind is seen as a "blank slate" at birth. The purpose of education is to fill that blank slate with facts, knowledge, philosophy, and an appreciation of liberty and freedom. Once the proper "data" are inserted into the brain, the individual will have learned to love truth, beauty, and justice. As new experiences impinge on each man, he will automatically process facts, weigh them in the balance, and choose what is best for himself and for his society. Education and rationality are thus the keystones in the Enlightenment Project to improve the human race.

The Lamp. An important Masonic symbol. Not only does it provide Physical illumination, but the light it provides represents spiritual and intellectual human development.

SIGNS AND SYMBOLS

We come now to a strange aspect of our story. It is true that Masonic lodges were dedicated to improving each member's moral and intellectual powers. What is strange is the method by which Freemasonry chose to impart its lessons. One would expect, given the Age's emphasis on logic, science, and rationality, that an appeal to the human intellect would be the method by which such lessons would be imparted. To the average person, formal classroom settings, or even a seminar-type discussion system, might be the obvious way to advance such an agenda. In the absence of any other ideas, perhaps a program of lectures might be considered appropriate. After all, Christian churches of all denominations had been using the "Homily," or sermon for hundreds of years to impart moral teachings. Surely this was a serviceable model?

What the new organization, dedicated to human reason chose to do was to institute procedures designed to appeal to the *emotional, irrational* side of human nature! Instead of seminars, discussion groups, or "Socratic Dialogues," Freemasonry teaches its philosophy with costumes, props, myth, interactive dramatics, and ceremonies designed to appeal to the senses. From the beginning, the Craft immersed its devotees in a complex system of theatrical productions designed to impress lessons upon the memory of its members. Lights, smells, bloody symbols, meditations on death, and appeals to the eternal human spirit were used from the start. A strange way, one would think, to reach the rational mind!

Early Masonic ceremony of the 1700's.*

In another part of this book we will cover Masonic ceremony in greater detail, but for the present, what is important is the *central paradox of Freemasonry.* Masonry seeks to reach the rational mind of man through irrational methods. It imparts lessons meant to be utilized by the intellect by tapping into the non-intellectual side of human nature. It seeks to train the individual to think for himself as a free creature, by using the emotional aspects of the brain and through a mysterious program of regimentation for its initiates.

Of course, initiatory experiences are as old as human society itself. Even primitive peoples have coming of age ceremonies, warrior fitness tests, and religious "mystery" cults, where knowledge is imparted to a small, spiritual elite. As far back in western history as ancient Greece, each *polis* had a network of ceremonies that each citizen was expected to pass through. One of the key background elements in the case against the philosopher Socrates was the knowledge that he had always refused to participate in the rites of Demeter and Persephone held at the cult center of Eleusis. He deemed them a mark of superstition and unworthy of a rational being.

One can make too much of this aspect of Freemasonry, since even the Greeks sought to excite the irrational in the search for truth. Still, the Brotherhood is one of the few modern institutions that continues this old, counterintuitive tradition of education.

THE MODERN MIND

Even during The Enlightenment, some thinkers were uncomfortable with the rationalistic view of the human mind. Edmund Burke most famously argued that prejudice is a natural outcome of society and that change is almost always problematical for groups.* He also had a great respect for tradition and a deep suspicion of rationalist schemes to improve society and the individual.

In the last thirty years or so, cognitive scientists have become convinced that the Enlightenment model of the human brain is *wrong*. For example, the classic view saw reason and emotion as opposed. Emotions got in the way of reason and interfered with rationality. However, research has shown that humans with brain damage that makes them incapable of experiencing emotion, or seeing it in others, cannot function rationally! They cannot perceive what decisions will lead to happiness or satisfaction—for themselves or anyone else.* Emotions actually *fuel* reason, rather than impairing its use.

Our mind (or rather what we consider our rational mind) is largely emotional, empathetic, uses metaphor to understand the world, and is shaped by experience, prejudice, and non-rational learning. Probably through luck, or because of its pre-Enlightenment roots, Freemasonry stumbled upon a perfect way to teach morality and self-development. Mysterious ceremony, strange symbols, memorized incantations, and other-worldly initiations, are at the core of the Masonic experience.

It is now time to explore just how the institution of Freemasonry was born and how it came to occupy its present position in the world.

The handshake—a very important Masonic symbol and sign of respect and brotherhood. Freemasons shake hands at almost every opportunity. There are several different kinds of handshakes and all depend on both men knowing a subtle code while clasping hands. This gesture symbolizes universal brotherhood and fellowship. It lies at the core of the Masonic experience.

Freemasons were not always held in high esteem. Detail from an engraving entitled "Night," by William Hogarth. A drunken Worshipful Master (head of his lodge) is being conducted home by another Mason. They are identified by their aprons, and the Master still wears his insignia of office. Drawing dates from 1738,

Greeting

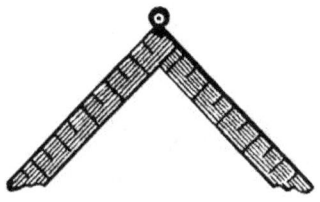

     After a lodge of Freemasons is opened in a formal way, the next item on the agenda is greeting any Masonic dignitaries, visiting brethren from other lodges or jurisdictions, and any new members of the lodge. Greetings are done in a very formal way and follow a set ritual. In the early 18th Century, many English lodges used the following formula: "The Right Worshipful Master and Fellows in that Right Worshipful Lodge from which we last came, greet you, greet you, greet you well." The proper reply from a visitor was: "God's good greeting be to you dear Brother."*

     The square is one of the most important tools in Freemasonry. It is the symbol of the Worshipful Master of each lodge (the presiding officer). He wears a small representation of the square around his neck attached to a velvet collar. The square is used to remind Freemasons to square their actions with the "square of virtue." Variations of this expression are still commonly used in English as in: "Are we square now? You are so square!" or "he treated me fair and square."

Freemasons in lodge after a Degree conferral. The three men dressed formally are lodge officers. The man in the suit has just received his Master Mason's Degree and is now a full member of the lodge.*

THE ORIGINS OF FREEMASONRY

Many works about Freemasonry open their section about its history with words to the effect that "the origins of the Craft are lost in the mists of time." That statement is true, but only up to a point. There actually *are* problems with Masonic history and we probably never will get a complete accounting of its origins, but basic facts are known. In recent years, a few Masonic researchers have done stellar work in researching where Freemasonry came from.

The story has been complicated until recently. First, the records of the Brotherhood have been lost or scattered over the centuries. Secondly, Freemasons have been a secretive group, keeping aloof from the outside world and hiding much of their institutional knowledge. Lastly, Masons have succeeded in confusing even themselves by conjuring up wild theories and legends about the origins of the movement. Until recently, the public has been left to grasp at mythology, half-baked history, or even outright fabrications when seeking information about the origins of the fraternity.

We know that Freemasonry had its public beginning on June 24, 1717, St. John the Baptist's Day, in London, England. On that date, four lodges within the city of London met at the Goose and Gridiron Ale House and formed the Grand Lodge of England. A Mr. Anthony Sayer, Gentleman, was chosen Grand Master, along with a slate of lesser officers. It is with this date that most modern histories of Freemasonry begin.* This fact alone is impressive. How many organizations are almost three hundred years old? There is an obvious question though. If Masonry was born on this date, where did the four lodges in London come from? They had to already have been in existence! They didn't just appear out of thin air did they? Logically, Freemasonry had to have already been established before the year 1717 if all the components of a Grand Lodge were *already* meeting and just ready to create the organization. So where did this organization come from?

Traditionally, Masonic writers have spun various theories about the origins of the Craft that trace its birth to several ancient—and sometimes glamorous—beginnings. Some have thought that it began with the medieval stone masons guilds in the Middle Ages. Others have claimed that Freemasons are the lineal descendants of the Order of Knights Templar dating back to the Crusades.* Finally, many early Masonic "scholars" have fallen back on a literal reading of the ritual, arguing that the beginning of Freemasonry dates to King Solomon's building of the Temple at Jerusalem.

The vast majority of such writings have had very little in the way of academic proof to recommend them. Hard facts have been generally nonexistent. Scholarship in recent years has been much more rigorous. Evidence found by current researchers paints a much more nuanced picture and advances a sophisticated set of explanations for the birth, and emergence in 1717, of Masonry.

In exploring the genesis of the order, it should be kept in mind that the modern world, as we know it, is relatively young. What that means is that the major tenants of Western Civilization are much newer, and more fragile, than we like to admit. Freedom of thought, association, and religion did not exist in a way that moderns would recognize just two hundred years ago. For that matter, most societies in the world today do not subscribe to the values of individual freedom and personal liberty. Another thing many tend to forget is that human progress is not always simple, straightforward, or even inevitable.

In school most of us learned that after the fall of the Roman Empire there was a period of barbarism, followed by the Middle Ages. Next came The Renaissance, The Enlightenment, the Romantic Age, and finally the modern world that we live in today. Everything is nice, neat, tidy, and progressive. There are no problems, or detours, and no backtracking. History is a triumphant story of inevitable development. Sorry, that is not the way mankind developed.

It is true that the Middle Ages *was* an era of saving and conserving the knowledge of the Ancient World. Using this fuel, The Renaissance *did* see an explosion of human progress in almost every intellectual field. Much Greek and Latin literature was rediscovered, higher education was invented in Italy and France, and art made a giant leap ahead and has seldom been equaled since. The beginning of what we now know as "the Scientific Method" also began to take shape in the Western mind.

Science, however, is a tricky business. Its basic goal is to explain the physical world—all of it. At issue is the fact that humans have always had problems reorienting explanations of reality. Thinking is hard. Changing ones' mind is painful. Who among us finds it exhilarating to find that our basic beliefs and assumptions need to be reexamined? Now extrapolate that feeling to an entire society. Human institutions become vested in viewing the world in a certain way. If anyone, or any movement, starts to challenge those assumptions, it is viewed as a threat. Threats to the established order need to be crushed.*

Socrates was one of the first figures in Western

history to find out about this process. He was put to death raising basic questions about truth, justice, and "the way things are." The technical charge was teaching the young disrespect for the Gods. A quick trial, and a nice drink of hemlock, solved this thorny problem for Athens. The process of discovery and questioning went on however.

Before any of us start feeling superior, we might want to look at the United States today. Think about such issues as the teaching of evolution, prayer in public schools, birth control access, civil rights for gay citizens, racial equality, and the constitutional issues associated with the "war on terror." Every society has its vested interests and blind spots. Progress is not a smooth, easy road. In this fact lies the birth of Freemasonry.

The Renaissance saw the beginnings of what became modern science. Scholars started to examine the natural world and explain its workings without the aid of superstition, dogma, and traditional thinking. Nicholas Copernicus advanced a theory that the sun was the center of the universe and the planets revolved around it. Galileo built on this theory by making observations with an early telescope, and started massing empirical data to support the Copernican view of the universe.

All well and good, one might suppose. A serious problem arose however. The Catholic Church had several hundred years of intellectual work invested the Aristotelian Theory of the universe which stated that the *earth*, not the *sun* was its center. Religious and political authority was wedded to this view. To make an extremely long story short, Galileo was hauled before the Holy Inquisition and made to publicly recant his beliefs about the universe and the bodies within it. He spent the rest of his life under house arrest. Recently, the Vatican has finally admitted that "mistakes were made" in this affair.* It must be pointed out that, at this time, no single church had a monopoly on intolerance. Martin Luther's views on the Copernican Theory were almost exactly the same as those of the Vatican. His solution was similar as well.

To be interested in science during the Renaissance was to be literally playing with fire. Galileo barely escaped the stake. A fellow Italian named Giordano Bruno was not so lucky. He was burned at the stake in 1600 in Rome after a church trial. A talented writer, philosopher, scientist, and theologian, Bruno's life illustrates the danger scholars could run into during this period. Today, investigators have had hundreds of years to separate "good" science from "bad." At the beginning of the process, it was impossible for even some of the greatest intellects to figure out what was what.

We now think of Sir Isaac Newton as the great thinker who invented calculus, discovered the laws of motion and gravity, and studied the spectrum of light. He also spent the last third of his life looking for hidden messages in the Bible so that he could predict the future. He wasted an inordinate amount of time trying to turn base metals into gold.* It's not that the line between magic, the occult, and science was blurred; the line didn't exist. At the dawn of science, everything was tried because unless something can be proven not to work, it can't be ruled out as useless.

It was this type of thinking that got Giordano Bruno in trouble. For example, if astronomical observations can provide data so that the movements of the heavenly bodies can be predicted, how do we know that the stars don't affect us here on earth? We now know (most of us) that astrology doesn't work. We also know that the Bible can't be used to predict the stock market. It took a long time for humans to figure out the divide between science and superstition. Bruno and his fellow thinkers were convinced that there was a hidden, underlying power in the universe that controlled everything. If man could discover this power, there would be no limit to what he could do here on earth. We now know that this "hidden power" is mathematics, but many of the Renaissance thinkers had something magical in mind.

In order to explore these exciting ideas, philosophers and students formed private *academies*, where like-minded thinkers could discuss, explore, and argue about new ideas and paradigms. New discoveries could also be presented. These academies were temporary, ad-hoc gatherings, sort of like discussion groups, or seminars. They started in Rome, but gradually spread to most major cities in Europe. Few lasted very long, and most were centered around one outstanding thinker, who organized the group. All were by invitation only. All were very, very private, for reasons that must be obvious by now. Whether you were in Rome, or London, or Germany, it didn't pay to advertise the fact that you and your friends were dabbling in science and philosophy.

To return to the story of Giordano Bruno. He led a very interesting, exciting, and dangerous life, constantly moving from place to place, trying to propagate his ideas. Born near Naples, Italy, he lived in Rome, Venice, Germany, Paris, and—what is interesting to Freemasons—in London from 1583 to 1585.* He was a sensation there publishing a minor scientific work, lecturing, arguing, and incidentally, forming an academy to help spread his world-views. His ideas of mysticism, hidden knowledge, and new learning spread through Elizabethan England. One influential enthusiast was William Schaw, Master of the Kings Works in Scotland.* Historians of Scottish Freemasonry have proven that Schaw played *the* major role in transforming Scottish stone craft guilds of workingmen into early forms of Masonic lodges.* Associations of stoneworkers provided a perfect "cover" for scholars and thinkers to meet and discuss the new learning. Freemasonry, as we know it, started in Scotland and was transplanted to England where it took root among existing medieval guilds.

Through the 1600's there are scattered references to Freemasonry in diaries, a few surviving lodge records, and in newspapers—particularly late in the century. During this period, the makeup of membership in Masonic lodges changed. Previously, lodges had been composed of stonemasons and laborers. Now membership began to consist of men with no connection to the building trades. The movement grew steadily and gathered strength until it burst into public view in 1717 in London.

ASIDE: GUILDS AND CATHEDRALS

Most standard examinations of Freemasonry include an elaborate treatment of the medieval craft system and then make an attempt to link those guilds of stone-workers to the birth of the Craft. They explain how the workers in the Middle Ages who built cathedrals were somehow "different," how their work was "mysterious" to those not in the building trades. In this way, Masonic writers also attempt to trace Masonic origins back through history to the ancient era of the Romans and Greeks.*

This technique originated in one of the very first widely distributed Masonic works: Dr. James Anderson's *The Constitutions of the Free-Masons* published in 1723 in London. It was the first all-purpose handbook for Freemasons and contained directions for constituting a lodge, as well as regulations and customs for the individual member to follow. Most importantly for our analysis, it also included an historical survey explaining how Freemasonry had come to be established.

Notre Dame Cathedral, Paris

Anderson wove a fanciful tale in which he began with Adam teaching his son Cain geometry, through Noah and his sons, to the Greeks, and Romans. Charles Martel, victor of the Battle of Tours in 732 is credited with helping to establish the Craft in England during the "Dark Ages."* These tales, while entertaining and interesting, seem to one observer at least, to contribute little to the field of Masonic studies. They should be left behind by scholars wishing to explore the Fraternity as they have no historic basis, and do little to elevate the subject. Indeed, it can be argued that such speculations have contributed to a lack of respect that Freemasonry has endured from serious researchers. It has only been in the last generation that Masonic studies have attracted mainstream academic practitioners.

FREEMASONRY SINCE 1717

As an important element of The Enlightenment, Freemasonry came into its own soon after its public unveiling. The whole orientation of the Craft had changed as well. Where before it had attracted scientists and mathematicians, or those interested in research, now it appealed to laymen with philosophic and political interests. The agenda of Freemasonry also became somewhat revolutionary—for its time.

England in the 1700's was a class-based society, with the monarch on top, then the aristocracy, and commoners at the bottom. Slaves, women, and those who did not subscribe to the Anglican faith, were non-persons. The Masonic Lodge offered an alternative society. Each lodge had a set of rules and regulations that members swore to uphold. Each member was equal to all other members within the confines of that lodge. The leadership was elected by all the members and their powers were restricted by the body's constitution. Every lodge was thus a mini-republic in a world that was ruled by force and privilege. This was a radical way of looking at the world for the time. Municipal police arrest records have been unearthed in Paris from the 1740's which accuse Freemasons of subverting the state by engaging in these "republican" activities.*

The Masonic movement swept through Europe in the first half of the 1700's. Citizens in many countries embraced Freemasonry, and almost every governing authority looked with suspicion on the new phenomenon. Freemasonry, since it was of English origin, naturally followed the flag and spread through the British Empire, where it made its way to North America and the Thirteen Colonies.

Freemasonry has had a varied reputation, and its influence has waxed and waned since the Eighteenth Century. In certain times, Freemasonry has even been used to support the established political order. In the 1700's, Emperor Joseph II of Austria used Masonic lodges as an element in his attempts to reform church and society within his kingdom.* Frederick the Great of Prussia had the same agenda and used Masonic lodges as a virtual arm of the state. In the Nineteenth Century, Freemasonry was often used by reformers and revolutionary movements to advance their goals. Garibaldi was a committed Brother and used his Masonic contacts in South America and Italy in his fight to help create the modern nation of Italy in the mid-1800's.*

In general, Freemasonry has continued its commitment to individual freedom, democratic ideals, and human development through the course of the Twentieth Century. It is instructive that in most countries where authoritarianism has become rooted, the government in power has taken steps to destroy the institution of Freemasonry. In Mussolini's Italy, Franco's Spain, Hitler's Germany, Hirohito's Japan, Lenin's Russia, Mao's China, Saddam's Iraq, North Korea, and in other places where liberty has been attacked, Freemasonry has been suppressed.* It has always however, risen like the mythical phoenix out the ashes.

Freemasonry's core remains in the English-speaking part of the world, particularly England and the United States. In the Twentieth Century Masonic membership has experienced several ups and downs. Beginning in 1900, Freemasonry experienced steady growth in the United States, reaching approximately 2 million members in 1930. This was roughly 9% of the white, male, adult population of the nation at the time. Soon after, Masonic membership declined due to the stress of the Great Depression. In the post-war period, the Craft again experienced a boom as U.S. membership peaked at around 4.15 million members in the year 1959.*

In recent decades, Masonic membership has declined significantly. In 2021, there were approximately 800,000 Masons in the United States. There are no complete statistics for world membership. Some have estimated that world-wide membership peaked at around 6 million members in 1960. An educated guess is that membership in 2021 was roughly 1.2 million men around the world. Unfortunately, there has been no indication recently that membership has stopped its decline. It is unclear to most observers when—or if—the trend will reverse itself.

The Masonic apron of Brother Meriwether Lewis. Lewis, is best known
for his leadership of the Lewis and Clark Expedition that explored
the territory of the Louisiana Purchase from 1804-1806. He was a committed
and enthusiastic Freemason for his entire adult life.

Minutes

After the Masonic lodge has formally opened, the "business of the lodge" gets underway. All regular gatherings of a social, political or private nature have a procedure of recording the activities and decisions of each meeting. Generally these are known as "minutes." Masonic gatherings are no different. Each lodge has an officer known as the Secretary. He takes minutes during all meetings, reads and sends all correspondence to and from the lodge, and generally keeps records of everything that happens.

As soon as a lodge meeting is underway, the first item of business is to read and approve the minutes of the previous meeting. This is when the Secretary plays his role as the archive of the lodge.

The Crossed Quills are the symbol of the Secretary. He wears a silver representation of them attached to his velvet collar as his badge office during meetings.

In some jurisdictions, the Worshipful Master and the other officers in a Masonic lodge wear formal dress during meetings. Full tuxedos with tails, white gloves, and black bow-ties are the norm. The Master wears a silk top hat as well. It is one of his badges of office. He is the only member that wears a hat during the proceedings.

FREEMASONRY TODAY

The average inquirer must be ready to burst at the seams by now. So far, this book has introduced the topic, given a historical sketch, talked about the psychology of the organization, and even given some inside information about the group. Most readers are much more impatient than writers would wish to admit. I've had talks with curious souls who have thrown up their hands in despair at my answers.

I remember one young man who got rather angry at me. To the best of my recollection he exploded in frustration. "You've talked about the history, you've given me some vague descriptions of meetings, and all you've done is beat around the bush! Just answer me this: what IS Freemasonry? Can't you just sum it up? Simply?"

It is now time that I attempt, in a reasonable number of pages, to answer that very question. But it can't be done simply, as you probably guessed. Where to begin? The very secrecy that Masons have invested so much in has made it extremely difficult to know where to even start.

Most of us have a point of reference when asking questions about a subject, even something we have no personal experience of. Although most of us have never been in the army or navy, the average person has *some* sort of idea in their heads about those institutions. Through books, news, or in films, an image has been imprinted within us as to what these institutions are and how they work. With Freemasonry, such handholds are scarce. Its purpose is vague. Good information is not accessible, even though lots of inflammatory data abound. Nevertheless, allow me to make a humble attempt.

Before starting however, one last caveat is needed. It must be emphasized that, while a world-wide entity, Freemasonry is very, very decentralized. Each country in which it is established is independent, and has customs and mores of its own. No one person, governing body, or written work speaks for the Craft. There is no Masonic "Bible," or handbook, in which a set of universal rules and regulations can be found. There are certain general principles however, which all Masons, in all countries, adhere to.

First, Freemasonry is a fraternal organization. It is made up entirely of male members. The etymology of the word "fraternity" derives from the Latin *frater* meaning "brother." As we have seen, the organization dates from the Eighteenth Century, long before modern ideas of sexual equality were formulated. The Fraternity has not changed with the times.

Second, Freemasonry is dedicated to the belief that men are capable of spiritual, moral, and intellectual improvement. Masonry provides the means for this growth process for its members.

Third, Freemasonry uses symbols, rituals, myths, and terms derived from the building trades to teach its lessons. The goal of this process is "building" a better man and helping him develop in moral, spiritual, and intellectual ways. Just as stoneworkers and other craftsmen built castles and cathedrals in the Middle Ages, so the individual Mason strives to foster personal growth and "build" a better person.

To join the Freemasons, an initiation ritual is

required. The process can be very elaborate and take several months. There are three distinct ceremonies that new members must participate in. They are called "degrees." Once a man has undergone all three initiations, he is a full member and is known as a "Master Mason."

Next, Freemasons meet in groups called "lodges." Often a lodge owns its own building, in which case the entire structure is known as a Masonic "temple."

In order to become a Freemason, a man must meet certain individual requirements. He must be of good moral character, he must be self-supporting, and he must believe in the existence of a "Supreme Being."

It is debatable what "good moral character" is, and various Masonic bodies around the world have differing standards. "Self-supporting" also is open to interpretation. At a minimum, it generally means being able to afford the initiation fees of one's lodge and the yearly dues to support its physical upkeep.

Belief in a "Supreme Being" is also an open question—up to a point. In order to become a Freemason, a man must believe in a unitary God, the organizing power of the universe, the source of all reality. As long as a new member can honestly swear that he believes in this concept, he has met the requirements of membership. Freemasonry has no interest in their member's personal definition of God. Christians of all denominations, Jews, Muslims, Hindus, Buddhists, Taoists, and even the adherents to Shintoism are all welcome.

Which brings us to the last aspect of our definition of Freemasonry: tolerance. Freemasonry is dedicated to "The Brotherhood of Man, under the Fatherhood of God."*

Politics, religious discussion, and any other topic that tends to divide mankind, is forbidden within the walls of the Masonic lodge. All are equal as Brethren, and all are dedicated to respecting their fellows and helping them to develop as humans.

This tradition of easygoing urbaneness in religious matters is an enduring legacy of The Enlightenment. An integral element of this period which saw the birth of the Masonic project was a hostility towards organized religion and its sects. In particular, dogmatic intolerance toward other beliefs was seen as anathema to a civilized society. Eighteenth century philosophers pointed to the horrors of Europe's Thirty Years War as the results of such religious prejudice.

As you can see, Freemasonry has a breathtaking, all-encompassing goal: to better the human race through the individual effort of each person. Masons believe that as a man strives to improve himself, the ripples from that effort will radiate outward and gradually make the world a better place. Because of this belief, Masonic lodges around the world are usually involved in volunteer and charitable work.

In the United States, the network of Shriners Hospitals provides an outlet for this impulse. Although they are associated in the popular mind with the more frivolous side of Freemasonry, Shriners Hospitals for children provide some of the finest medical care for children at virtually no cost to patients or their families. They are entirely supported by donations and trust funds set up by the Masonic movement in the early 20th Century. It is possible that this system is unequaled anywhere else.

ANGLO-AMERICAN TRADITIONS

With the creation of the Grand Lodge of England in 1717, Freemasonry "followed the flag" as Great Britain expanded its influence and created an empire that reached into every corner of the globe. Masonic lodges sprang up in colonies and overseas posts, particularly attracting members from government officials, military officers, and leading citizens.

In this early period, the rules and regulations were very fluid. Lodges were not required to meet in a single, purpose-built address. Many met in taverns or inns, renting a single room for one evening only. British army regiments instituted so-called "traveling lodges" that met wherever the unit was stationed. Although the Brotherhood has spread all over the world, the legacy of this period gives modern Freemasonry a distinctively "Anglo-American" feel. The decentralization of Freemasonry has been an integral element right from its birth. As previously mentioned, the Grand Lodge of England was formed on June 24, 1717 in London. This event was the culmination of a long process that brought Freemasonry into being. Anthony Sayer was elected Grand Master. Little is known about him except that he was titled "Gentleman" in the official minutes. This fact seems to indicate that, while Sayer was a committed and respected Freemason, he had little prestige or status within London society.*

In an effort to increase its popularity and *cachet*, the Grand Lodge began accepting members of the nobility as brethren. On June 24, 1721, Lord Stanhope, Earl of Chesterfield was made a Mason and the Duke of Montague was elected Grand Master. In 1723, the Duke of Wharton assumed office. Under the leadership of aristocrats such as these, members with less exalted backgrounds felt left out. Complaints began to be aired about declining standards for membership. Ritualistic work soon became neglected. Freemasonry seemed to be in danger of turning into a rich man's drinking club. By 1738, under the leadership of Lord Byron, the Craft seemed headed for oblivion.*

It was during this period that an insurgent movement arose in London which was to transform the entire Fraternity. In 1751, Laurence Dermott, an Irish housepainter, formed "The Grand Lodge of 'Antient' Masons" in London. Charging that the current Grand Lodge had wrongly instituted "Modern" changes to ritual and customs, he led a revival to restore purity and equality to Masonry. Most of Dermott's charges were true. Ritual *was* being neglected, and the organization *was* becoming too elitist in its membership. "Antient" Masonry aimed to restore the Craft to its original form and intent. As part of this effort, Dermott published a new handbook of rules and regulations to replace the casual set of customs that had arisen in the organization.

This insurgent movement spread through the Masonic world like wild-fire and membership soared among the newly emerging middle-class of the Eighteenth Century. The authority of the English Grand Lodge came under assault from other quarters as well. In an effort to assert itself, it granted charters to Irish lodges in order to form the Grand Lodge of Ireland. A similar effort in

Scotland met a cool reception. Given the older traditions of the North, the Scots felt that they had no need of a "blessing" from their English Brethren. The existing lodges formed the Grand Lodge of St. John of Scotland in 1736.*

Soon even the original Grand Lodge of England had given up and began calling itself the "Modern" form of Masonry. Through the rest of the Eighteenth Century, leaders of both groups tried to negotiate a peace. By 1813, the battle finally ended in s stalemate. The two Grand Lodges merged and became "The United Grand Lodge of Ancient Freemasons of England." With internecine war over, English Freemasonry became mostly a more middle-class phenomenon, with a much greater attention to ritualistic workings. The "peace" within the Fraternity has held firm and few internal problems have arisen. As a courtesy however, and in keeping with British norms, a member of the Royal family is elected Grand Master—the titular head of the entire Grand Lodge.

In the United States, the story of Freemasonry has been much more complex—with exciting ups and downs, coupled with national prejudices and social unrest. During the colonial period lodges were formed by groups within each of the original thirteen colonies. The authority to do so came from "warrants" (permission) from the Grand Lodge of England.

With the advent of the American Revolution, lodges in each of the newly independent colonies formed their own state-based Grand Lodges. All declared their Masonic independence and were duly recognized as separate and equal by the Grand Lodge of England. This curious process was expedited by the fact that Masonry in

British Isles was apolitical and took no nationalistic position during the military conflict.

The same could not be said for Freemasonry in the new United States. During the Revolutionary War, the Craft played an important role in helping to solidify the political and military leadership of the rebellious colonies. Although it cannot be categorically stated that Freemasonry played a leading role in forming the Revolutionary temperament of the time, it *did* serve to reinforce the bonds among the officers in Washington's army , and within the fledgling national government.*

With the war over, American Freemasonry began to diverge from its English roots. Consciously, or unconsciously, it imitated the new Federal system of the new nation. There were brief attempts to establish a unitary Masonic organization, but they quickly failed. American Freemasonry adopted a state-oriented structure and has never changed. Each of the Original Thirteen States formed its own grand lodge. As the nation grew, with settlers heading west, they took Freemasonry with them, usually from the nearest adjacent grand lodge. When a territory achieved statehood, it normally organized its own Masonic Grand Lodge and declared its independence. In this way, Freemasonry spread throughout the United States. At the present time, there are 51 Grand Lodges, one for each state and one for the District of Columbia.

Through the first quarter of the 1800's, Freemasonry in the United States experienced a "golden age." By almost every measure the Brotherhood played a dominant role in American civic life. The cornerstone laying ceremonies of the U.S. Capital building and the

White House were Masonic in nature. Most public buildings across the country were also dedicated with Masonic rites. Many public leaders were Freemasons—at least it seemed so to many observers. In 1824, President James Monroe, Speaker of the House Henry Clay, and Chief Justice John Marshall were all active Masons. At the local level Masonic influence seemed pervasive. The United States could almost have been termed a "Masonic Republic." No one would have predicted that Freemasonry was about to enter an era of crisis.

THE MORGAN AFFAIR

In western New York State during the year 1826, occurred a series of events known to history as "The Morgan Affair." William Morgan, a Masonic imposter and ne'er-do-well, attempted to publish an *expose*` of the ritual. He was arrested on trumped up charges, kidnapped from the county jail, and disappeared. Most local officials were Freemasons. After twenty trials and three special prosecutors, only a handful of convictions were obtained. At the very least, obstruction of justice had occurred due to Masonic influence. Public outrage was so great that a new movement was born almost overnight: Anti-Masonry.*

The movement embodied two criticisms of Freemasonry that had festered beneath American society for some time. Many felt that Masonry was elitist and incompatible with the ideals of a free republic. There were also religious objections that it subverted Christianity itself, particularly with its oaths and obligations. The nation was in grave danger morally and politically. Only when Freemasonry was utterly destroyed could citizens breathe easily again.

Anti-Masonry spread like wild-fire throughout the

States and was particularly strong in the northern half of the United States. Hundreds of newspapers were founded and a political party created. Candidates won office at all levels running as Anti-Masons. Under public pressure, Freemasons quit the Brotherhood in droves. In Michigan and Vermont, Masonry ceased to operate at all. By the late 1830's, the movement had burned itself out and had merged with other political movements.* The damage to the Fraternity had been done by then however, and took years to heal.

State by state, Masonic leaders kept a low profile and struggled to keep their individual organizations alive. As the national conflict over slavery took center stage during the *antebellum* period Freemasons increasingly came to be seen as unimportant. Gradually, the health of the movement improved. After the Civil War, Freemasonry experienced a boom period all around the nation. Clubs, veterans groups, and civic organizations became very popular in American Society.

MODERN STATE OF AFFAIRS

The Twentieth Century was a roller coaster ride for Freemasonry in the United States and in North America. Masonic growth was steady until it exploded in the period after World War II. Membership reached a peak in 1960, but then experienced a steady decline that continues to the present time. The following chart tells the story of the rise and fall of membership numbers in the last one hundred years. Although only concerned with membership in the United States, the figures on membership in Canada are not healthy either.

UNITED STATES

Year	Population	Freemasons	Pop	Males
1900	75,994,575	920,459	1.2%	2.4%
1940	131,669,275	2,457,263	1.8%	3.6%
1960	179,323,175	4,099,219	2.3%	4.6%
1990	248,709,873	2,531,643	1%	2 %
2000	281,421,906	1,841,169	.7%	1.4%
2009	300,000,000	1,404,059	.5%	1 %
2023	334,253,854	869,429	.26%	.52 %

Historically, world-wide Masonic membership has approximated the growth of North America. Despite the spread of Freemasonry all over the world in the latter half of the Twentieth Century, the future of the Fraternity looks challenging to most observers.

Previous page: the passage of time. An illustration of an old Masonic allegory. A virgin stands before a broken column, reading a book, and holding a branch of acacia. Behind her is a representation of Father Time leaning on his scythe, and with an hourglass at his feet. He is counting the strands of the girl's hair.

An obvious interpretation of this scene is that all human endeavors eventually fall into ruin. Indeed, youth, beauty, and all life are subject to the rules of the universe and must eventually grow old, decay, and die.

The acacia tree is a type of pine found in the Middle East. Like its cousin the Evergreen, it represents not only memory and hope for the future, but it can also stand for the promise of a future state of being after this earthly life ends.

Communications

Once a lodge has been formally opened and underway, the Secretary rises and begins the normal order of business. Like any meeting, after reading the minutes, the next thing to be done is reading any and all communications to the group. These can range from letters announcing get-togethers or invitations from neighboring lodges, to formal letters from the Grand Master of the state directing all Freemasons under his authority to follow a certain course of conduct. Often petitions for membership are read at this stage of the meeting.

The level is another important tool in Freemasonry. It is the symbol of the Senior Warden of a lodge. He could be termed the vice-president of the organization. He wears a small representation of the level around his neck attached to a velvet collar. The level reminds the Freemason that we are all traveling upon the "level of time towards an undiscovered country from which no traveler returns."

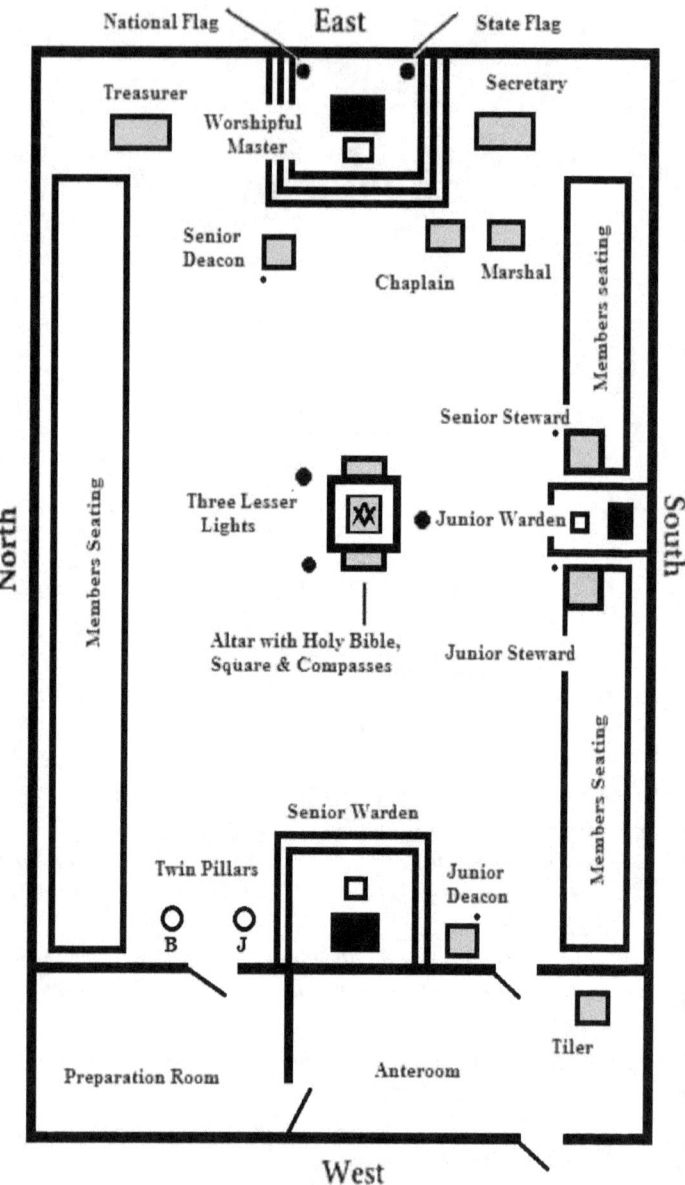

A MASONIC LODGE ROOM

Freemasons spend much of their active fraternal life in lodge buildings, most particularly in the lodge room itself. In fact, when most Masons talk of "going to lodge" they are speaking about the time spent within the closed, private space that is their special room. In it, the regular meetings are conducted. New applicants go through the initiation ceremonies inside. Also, men petitioning for membership are voted upon there. At the end of a Brother's life, lodge rooms are the place where memorial services may be conducted at the request of the family. In short, the lodge room lies at the heart of the Masonic experience.

The reader may ask why there is a diagram of the room contained in this work? Aren't all the workings of Freemasonry secret? Are outsiders even permitted to learn about this sacred space? How can this be?

The answer to these questions is very simple. Freemasonry is a *private* organization, but it is not a *secret* society. Lodge buildings are open to the public. Many grand lodges permit public tours to be conducted inside local Masonic temples. Although there are certain aspects of the ritual that are not to be divulged, by the end of this chapter the average questioner will have most of his curiosity satisfied as to what actually happens in the Lodge.

First, we must start with the room, its geography, the officers of the lodge, their jobs, and where they do their work. The lodge room is meant to be a miniature representation of the Temple of Solomon at Jerusalem. There is an altar, three officers that supervise "the work," and furnishings used during degrees.

Let's start with basics. The lodge room has four sides; East, West, North, and South. These have nothing to do with geography, however. Lodge buildings are not oriented in any particular direction. The north side of the lodge room seldom points to "true north." The **East** is where the Worshipful Master presides over the meeting. Many other officers have their places there. During a meeting, the attention of the Brethren will usually be focused toward the East. The **West** end is the second most important side of the room. This is where a second group of officers sit. This is also where the entrance to the lodge room is. The **South** side is where one final officer sits. The **North** side contains no officers, just regular seating.

This lodge design is a typical one found in many states in North America. It must be emphasized however, that Freemasonry has no single, standard design for a lodge room. The essentials are everywhere the same, but details may differ from state to state, and country to country. As we explore the room you will need to consult the diagram on page 58.

A representation of King Solomon's Temple, or "the First Temple." This is the "Holy of Holies," the building within the Temple compound that supposedly housed the Ark of the Covenant. Its entrance was flanked by two brazen pillars named "Boaz," and "Jachin." The Temple figures large in Masonry because the story of its construction is used in the ritual.*

The **Anteroom** is the last "public" space in the lodge. No one but Freemasons can proceed beyond this area. This is where Brethren sign in, put on their aprons, and generally socialize with each other before meetings start.

There is another very important room that opens off of the Anteroom: the **Preparation Room.** This room is used by candidates to get ready to receive their Masonic degrees. In it, men are divested of their everyday garb and put on the costume in which they will be initiated into the Fraternity.

Moving from the vestibule through the **Inner Door**, we come into the **Lodge Room** proper. The first thing that usually catches one's eye is the **Holy Altar**.

Symbolically, it represents the central place that the Creator should have in your life. Remember that a requirement of membership is the belief in a Supreme Being. Freemasons don't care what denomination—or religion—a man belongs to, just that he believes in a power greater than mankind. The Masonic term for this creator is "The Great Architect of the Universe," or the G.A.O.T.U.

Upon the Altar are the three "Great Lights" of Freemasonry: the Holy Bible, Square, and Compasses. In

North America most lodges use the Holy Bible since society is overwhelmingly Judeo-Christian in composition. This situation is changing however and, in the future, many "Sacred Books" from other religious traditions will be increasingly found on Masonic altars. When a meeting is in progress, the Bible must be open and when the Holy Book is closed, the meeting is over. Around the Altar are the three "Lesser Lights." They represent the sun, the moon, and the Master of the lodge. When a lodge is meeting, they are lit. When the meeting is over, they are extinguished. More about these lights later. There is general seating for members on the North and South sides of the room. Now that you have an idea of the geography of the lodge, let's move on to the officers within it.

OFFICERS OF THE LODGE

At the East end of the lodge is a raised platform which has three steps. On top of this platform is a dais upon which are three chairs, and a waist-high pedestal.

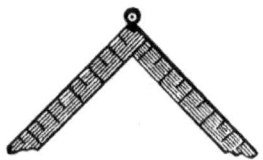

This is the station of the **Worshipful Master (WM)**. The Master is the president, if you will, of the lodge. He is elected for a one-year term and is responsible for everything concerning that lodge. He presides over meetings, he is on every committee, and he plans all major activities for that year. He is to be obeyed in all matters, although his power is not absolute. He does most of the speaking during regular meetings. Around his neck is his jewel of office: the square.

The Master is addressed as "worshipful," or "most worshipful," because it is an old English form of respect, similar to "honorable," or "your honor." In front of the Master's chair is a pedestal. On it are his gavel, a stone upon which he gavels meetings to order, and some additional Masonic tools. Somewhere on the East wall, in a frame, is the Warrant and Constitution of the lodge. This is the paper issued by the state Grand Lodge creating the lodge and authorizing it to meet. Many are very old, some dating back to the 1800's or even earlier. The Warrant must be displayed during meetings for the lodge to legally meet. If the building were to burn down, the first thing to be saved should be the Warrant and Constitution.

The Master sits while he presides over the meeting and he also wears a hat. In some parts of the world it is a formal, top hat. In other, more relaxed jurisdictions a fedora, a cowboy hat, or even a baseball cap are worn. Clothing varies as well. Some state Grand Lodges mandate a tuxedo, complete with tails, for lodge officers. Regular members wear suits, or at least coats and ties. In many midwestern parts of the United States, ties are rare and officers dress casually—even in t-shirts and blue jeans.

At the opposite end from the Master, in the West end of the room, is the seat of the second-ranking member of the lodge, the **Senior Warden (SW)**. The Senior Warden could be termed the vice-president of the lodge. He is also elected for a one-year term and is responsible for supporting and assisting the Master. He presides over meetings if the Master is absent. He is dressed similarly to the Worshipful Master except that he wears no hat. Around his neck is his jewel of office: the level. Except in very rare instances, the Senior Warden is the "heir apparent" and will succeed the Master during the next year. He has a pedestal similar to the Master's with similar implements upon it.

One additional element to the Senior Warden's station is a miniature column that rests upon his pedestal. He uses it in opening and closing lodge ceremonies and to signal to the brethren when the meeting is open or closed.

On the South side of the lodge room is a small platform where the **Junior Warden (JW)** sits. He is the third ranking member of the lodge. He too serves a one-year term and is responsible for supporting and assisting the Senior Warden and the Master, in any way he can. He presides over meetings if the Senior Warden and the Worshipful Master are absent. He is dressed similarly to the other two ranking officers. Around his neck is his jewel of office: the plumb. His pedestal is similar to the other two, and he also has a column which he uses to help open and close meetings.

If the meeting recesses for a short time, he is responsible for keeping order in the room. He will normally be elected Master in two years.

At the North East corner of the lodge room is the desk of the **Treasurer (TREA)**. He is the fourth ranking member of the lodge and is also annually elected by the membership. Around his neck is his jewel of office: the crossed keys. His duties are of course, financial. He is responsible for keeping the books and seeing that the finances of the lodge are in good order. He is one of the officers that countersigns all checks for the payment of goods and services. The other signees are the Secretary and the Worshipful Master. He gives a report to the membership during every meeting detailing income, expenses, payments, and the overall cash balance of the lodge. Although technically anyone is eligible to run for this office, because of the work, responsibility, and trust involved, a long-time member of the lodge, is usually elected. Often he has been Worshipful Master. In many lodges, Treasurers serve for multiple terms. Since no lodge positions are paid, there is never very much competition for the duties and responsibilities of this position.

At the South East corner is the desk of the **Secretary (SEC)**, the fifth ranking officer of the lodge. He wears the crossed quills as his jewel of office. He is responsible for keeping the minutes of all meetings. The Secretary helps compose, and mail, the monthly meeting notices. He is the point of contact for all correspondence from the Grand Lodge. All notices, changes of rules, and decisions or edicts from the Grand Lodge, come to his desk. He reads the minutes from the previous meetings, he coordinates degrees, he makes sure that membership cards are mailed out, that candidates are vetted—in short, the secretary does *all* the paperwork of the lodge. Like the

Treasurer, in most lodges he is a Past Worshipful Master and is a repository of lodge wisdom and custom. He is the strong right arm and support of the Master. It is no exaggeration to say that the Secretary is probably the most important member of the lodge. Any Freemason will tell you that if you have to choose between the Master, or the Secretary suddenly dropping dead, it is better if the Master goes! Like the other officers, his term is for one year, but usually lodges refuse to let a good secretary retire. Most serve for many years.

The next two officers have similar duties. Looking toward the East, in front of, and to the right of the Worshipful Master, is the **Senior Deacon (SD)**. Looking toward the West, on the right hand of the Senior Warden, is the **Junior Deacon (JD)**. Both officers wear a jewel featuring the square and compasses—the basic symbol of Freemasonry. In the center of the Senior Deacon's jewel is the sun. In the center of the Junior Deacon's is the moon. Both carry messages and perform varied jobs during the stated meeting. The Senior Deacon carries messages for the Worshipful Master—usually to the Senior Warden. In Masonic lore, just as the sun rules the day, the Worshipful Master rules the lodge—hence the sun symbol. The Junior

Deacon carries messages within the lodge for the Senior Warden—usually to the Junior Warden. As the Senior Warden is junior to the Master, his is sometimes likened to the moon which rules the night—the lesser part of the day. As they perform their messenger duties, both men carry a seven foot long staff—or wand—in their right hands. Neither officer is elected. The Senior Deacon is however, normally slated to move up to Junior Warden the following year. The Junior Deacon normally will move up to the Senior Deacon's position. A final duty of the Junior Warden is answering the door to the lodge room. There are occasions when a member comes to a meeting late, or a visitor arrives unexpectedly. In order to gain admission to a meeting, the Brother must knock on the door, identify himself and ask permission to enter. The Junior Warden relays these requests and admits anyone who is entitled to enter during a meeting.

In many jurisdictions the Junior Deacon also meets new candidates in the preparation room, helps them get ready for the initiation ceremonies, and assists the Senior Deacon in escorting them around the lodge room in the course of the ceremony.

Both of these officers have made a commitment to "moving up the line" and someday having the opportunity to become the Worshipful Master. As an officer moves up to more senior positions in the lodge, he plays a more and more important role in the ceremonies and rituals of Masonry.

The next two officers sit on either side of the Junior Warden in the South. On his right hand is the **Senior Steward (SS)**. On his left is the **Junior Steward (JS)**.

Both officers wear a jewel around their necks that features a cornucopia—a "horn of plenty." The horns are filled with fruits and vegetables and spill out in profusion. They represent the fruits of labor or, in other words, the rewards of a job well done.

Both are appointed officers and serve for one year. The Senior Steward is charged with assisting the Junior Warden in any way he can. He is also responsible for taking the place of the Junior Warden should that officer be unable to attend a meeting.

The Junior Steward is charged with assisting the Senior Steward and the Junior Warden. He is responsible for taking the Senior Steward's place if that officer is absent. Both stewards are "jacks of all trades" and assist the other, more senior officers in the lodge. Depending on the customs in different states, the Stewards alone have the responsibility of meeting candidates in the preparation room.

In the East side of the lodge, almost directly in front of the Secretary's desk, is the place of the officer known as the **Marshall (MA)**. His jewel is the crossed batons. The Marshall is the Lodge's master of ceremonies, or the conductor and supervisor of the rituals that the group performs. He is an appointed officer and is usually an experienced Brother. His job becomes vital when groups of distinguished Masonic visitors or dignitaries attend the lodge meeting. It is his job to see that protocols are observed, that correct precedence and etiquette are followed.

There is one more officer left within the lodge room, and he plays a small, but vital, role in all Masonic gatherings. His chair is in front, and to the left of, the Worshipful Master's station, between the Senior Deacon and the Marshall. He is the **Chaplain (CH)**. He wears a small open book as his jewel of office. It normally represents the Holy Bible, but remember that *any* sacred text can be used within the lodge, depending on one's religion. Christianity and Freemasonry are *not* synonymous, although in many lodges are generally made up of Christian members.

The Chaplain's duties are to lead the lodge in

prayer during the opening and closing ceremonies. He also recites a prayer during the First Degree when a Candidate is made a Freemason. Prayers are also usually a part of any additional lodge ceremony not connected with regular meetings. Finally, when a brother's family requests a Masonic funeral, the Chaplain leads the lodge in paying a last tribute to the deceased. Prayers during Masonic gatherings are generally addressed to "The Great Architect of the Universe."

The Chaplain is an appointed office for one year. In lodges with members who happen to be clergymen, it is often the case that they are usually asked to fill this chair. Any member of the lodge, however, is eligible.

We now come to the loneliest of all the officers that serve the lodge: the **Tiler (TIL)**. His jewel of office, which also hangs around his neck, is the sword. He also carries a real one. He guards the door that separates the Anteroom from the lodge room itself. He is also in charge of greeting visitors to the lodge before meetings, and making sure that they sign in. He determines if they can be vouched for, or if they need an examination. He is also in charge of making sure that the aprons of the lodge are available in the lobby for the use of lodge members. During the meetings of the lodge, the Tiler stays outside and secures the entrance, making sure that no unauthorized persons come near. An informal role of most Tylers is to make sure that the dining area is ready for use after the meeting. If any food is cooking he also makes sure to give it a stir so that nothing burns!

After each Masonic meeting comes the fellowship hour where refreshments and food are served in the lodge's dining room. In the opinion of most Freemasons, this period is just as important as the actual meeting itself. This is a time for brethren to relax, get something to eat, gossip, talk about the meeting, or the lodge in an informal way. This is an important time when the bonds of brotherly love and affection are strengthened.

Finally, lodge usually have three annually elected **Trustees**. They are charged with overseeing the business and financial health of the lodge. They are usually brethren who have served as Worshipful Master in the past and wish to continue to serve the organization. They vaguely resemble a board of directors. The Secretary, Treasurer, and Worshipful Master do not answer to them and they do not instruct those officers. They can best be understood as a legal protection for the lodge organization, and as an additional source of oversight and institutional wisdom.

A LODGE MEETING

At this point, perhaps it would be useful to explore what happens at a typical meeting. If nothing else, this might help you understand what goes during a meeting and the purposes of the actions taken during the gathering. You will see that a typical Masonic meeting is unremarkable.

First, the formal name for a regular meeting is "The Monthly Stated Meeting." It is called that because it will be *stated* in the monthly notice that the lodge secretary sends to all members. Traditionally, notices are sent by mail, although recently some grand lodges have begun to encourage the use of email. Printing and mailing costs add up to large sums of money and could be better used in other, more beneficial ways. Notices must be sent so that they are received by members well ahead of meetings—usually a week.

Notices have a common form. Usually they contain four pages. On the front is the name and number of the lodge and its founding date. On the back cover are listed all the officers and committees of the lodge, along with a list of living Past Masters. On page two is the program of that month's meeting, or meetings. If Degrees are being conferred, an "Extra Stated Meeting" will be held and that date will be included. The full names and addresses of anyone petitioning to join the lodge will also be in the notice. This is a requirement from most grand lodges. Finally, any special announcements or messages are included. A membership progress report for the year will list membership numbers, deaths, and any other losses up to the present date.

Meetings are standardized. The agenda normally consists of the opening ceremony, greeting of visitors, reading of minutes, communications, announcements, the program for the evening, reports of committees, reading and payment of any bills with the Treasurer's report, and the closing ceremony.

At the proper time (usually 7 PM or 7:30), the Worshipful Master calls the lodge to order, and directs the ceremony to "Tile" the lodge. Tile means to close all doors and make sure that they are guarded so that intruders cannot approach. The lodge is now cut off from the outside—*profane*—world. Then the opening ceremony is conducted, and the Holy Bible opened on the Altar. After a Flag ceremony featuring the Pledge of Allegiance, visitors to the lodge are greeted and welcomed.

Next, the minutes of the previous meeting (or meetings) are read by the Secretary, and approved by the members. Letters, announcements, or any other communications to the lodge are also read to the assembled Brethren at this time. Then any petitions for membership are announced. A committee is appointed to investigate petitioners, and report back to the lodge. If investigations have been completed, the potential member is voted on by the Brethren at this point in the meeting. A ballot box is placed upon the Altar and a vote taken.

Most lodges have a program for the evening—a special event, speaker, or a presentation of some sort. It is at this point in the evening that it would take place. Next, any reports of the standing committees are given and any problems, or actions needed, are discussed.

Finally, bills are read, the Treasurer gives a report on the financial health of the lodge, and the closing ceremony is performed. The Bible is then closed.

On one level, it *is* simply a meeting like any other. It can be boring. It is somewhat like paying bills, and filing personal financial records. Not real compelling, but necessary. What can't be expressed on paper is the stateliness, the dignity, the magic, if you will, of the meeting. Masonic gatherings are filled with stylized behavior. The language used by the officers, the mannerisms of the Brethren when they address the Master, the voting procedures—all are done according to a severe ritualistic code. When entered into with understanding and an open frame of mind, one can learn a lot about oneself, and one's fellow Masons.

There are slightly differing customs and manners in different states and jurisdictions. In some states the opening ceremonies can last one half hour or more. The same can be said for the closing rituals. The core of the meeting, the absolute requirements of the ritual, are the same everywhere. I have participated in Masonic meetings in more than a few jurisdictions. The venues have ranged from massive, five story stone and marble edifices in large cities, to small, wooden buildings located in the country. I have seen some lodges that have sophisticated light, sound, and heating and cooling systems. I have sat in lodges that had no heat or air conditioning at all. The outward trappings do not concern Freemasons. What is important is the spirit of the membership and their commitment to the practice of brotherly love for all mankind. That never changes, no matter how grand, or how mean, the setting.

But these regular meetings, these hum-drum boring gatherings, are not what readers wish to explore. What about the degrees? What about the weird, strange cermonies? It is now time to reveal what Freemasons "really" do in their temples.

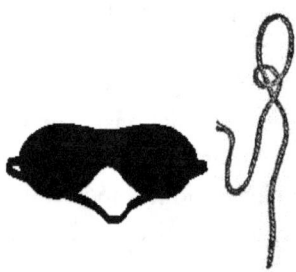

A blindfold and a rope. The rope is called a "cable tow,"Both are used in the Masonic ceremonies of initiation. Their use and purpose will be explored in the next chapter.

Business

  Once a lodge has been formally opened and the normal order of business has been dispatched, other more important items can be addressed. Foremost among these is holding a vote on new admissions to the lodge. Anyone wishing to join must petition a lodge and submit to an anonymous vote of the members present that night. In most jurisdictions, one dissenting vote is sufficient for rejection. Freemasons use a ballot box filled with white and black marbles. Members vote by using white for acceptance, black for rejection, hence the term "black balled."

  The plumb is another important tool in Freemasonry. It is the symbol of the Junior Warden of a lodge. He wears a small representation around his neck as his badge of office. The plumb reminds the Freemason that he should be upright before God and man and do nothing base to disgrace himself or Freemasonry.

Entered Apprentice Apron. Worn with the flap turned up. Originally this was thought to protect the wearer from dirt, tools, and building materials that the beginning apprentice worker would have to carry in the course of helping more experienced workmen.

THE FIRST DEGREE

At last we will begin to explain, as far as possible what those Freemasons actually *do* in their lodges. The answer is simple—but also complex. What Freemasons do is confer degrees on new members and thereby instruct them in the "mysteries" of the Craft. The ceremonies are very long, solemn affairs, with much symbolism and rhetorical language. The ultimate purpose is to teach morality and wisdom through repetition, ritual, and reaching *beyond* the rational intellect of the individual to the spiritual side of the candidate.

One more note here about secrecy. Again, while Freemasonry is a private organization, it is incorrect to consider it a secret society, with all aspects of it to be forever concealed from others. Our buildings are clearly marked by signs. Membership lists can be obtained through Grand Lodge records. Most of our facilities are available for rent to the general public. Many lodges actually have "open houses" where tours are given to anyone who wishes to learn more about Freemasonry. The only things truly secret concerning Masonic ritual are the *specific* language used in it, the passwords, the grips and the special signs associated with each degree. These are sacrosanct, but everything else can be revealed to outsiders. Most of the ritual can be found on the internet or in a good public library. The real secrets of Freemasonry are within each brother's soul. Let's begin with the First Degree—the Entered Apprentice Mason's Degree.

A masonic degree consists of six parts: the preparation, the circumambulation, the obligation, the investiture, and the charge. We will take each of the degrees in turn and explore their structure and the symbolism contained within them.

I was much like the "average" candidate when I arrived at my lodge almost twenty years ago for my first degree. Of course at the time, I didn't know what it was called, all I really knew was that I was going to join the Masons that night. I arrived in my best suit with a check for my dues and initiation fees and a case of nerves. Like many men, I didn't really know much about what I was getting into. My grandfather had been a member, and we kept his old Shriners' fez and a Scottish Rite ring with the family keepsakes. I remember looking at them as a child and wondering about their significance. All I knew was that George Washington had been a Freemason, and that some of my friends and acquaintances were enthusiastic about the organization. I figured the only way to find out was to join. There had to be something worthwhile there. I had the money, the curiosity, and the spare time, so why not try it?

In spite of my resolution, I remember very well some of my emotions from that night: nervous anticipation, puzzlement, awkwardness, pride, and some feelings of embarrassment.* I was able to conquer these feelings and continue on. This resolution itself is one of the first lessons impressed upon the new Freemason. All of us, at one time or another, have spoken about "getting past one's fears," or "trusting in others when faced with the unknown." How many people actually *experience* this however? All Masonic Brethren have. This alone forms a powerful bond between Masons. It builds a relationship that stays strong and is always remembered. Freemasons are often derided for their comradery. Critics charge that it is false. It is not credible that complete strangers should become friends in a matter of minutes when meeting. Those who scoff at such things are wrong. The initiation ceremonies that all Freemasons have experienced are the key and the "secret" to this sense of brotherhood. Let us continue, however with the first step in Masonry—called the Entered Apprentice Degree.*

The Preparation. The degree process begins when the candidate enters the lodge building and is taken in hand by an experienced Brother, sometimes known as a Guide. After a few preliminaries in the Anteroom, he is taken to the Preparation Room to get ready physically and spiritually for his entrance into the Masonic brotherhood.

Under the direction of his Guide, the Candidate removes most of his clothing and dons a special blue garment that resembles a set of pajamas. He abandons all his money and takes off any valuable items that he normally wears. He removes all metal objects from his person. He is barefoot and puts a slipper on his right foot. His pant leg is rolled up so that his left knee is bare. A rope—or cable tow—is knotted and wound once around his neck. Finally, he dons a blindfold—in Masonic terms, a "hoodwink." He is thus blind, helpless, defenseless, penniless, and isn't even wearing his own clothes!

The reason a Candidate is prepared this way is to teach him about certain aspects of Freemasonry. You can't buy your way into Masonry, no matter how much money you have. The lodge is a place of peace, so any metal objects which could be used as weapons must be put aside. He wears a special outfit so that he is, in a sense, anonymous and without the advantages of wealth, fame, or social position. The purpose of the cable tow is to reinforce his helplessness in the face of the unknown. It is held by the Guide and is used to control his actions while in the lodge room. The blindfold is to teach him that he is spiritually blind, and that he is seeking "Masonic Light."

Once he is all ready, the Candidate waits in the Preparation Room with his Guide, listening to the muffled sounds of a meeting getting underway. Silence usually reigns in this little room as the Candidate contemplates what might happen next. When the proper time arrives, his hand is guided to a door knocker which he uses to knock three times in order to gain admission. His Guide speaks for him and tells whoever asks that a poor, blind, candidate for Freemasonry begs to be admitted and introduced into its mysteries. After his Guide gives the pass-word, the Candidate is then led into the darkened lodge room, told to kneel, and then is asked two questions. First, he is asked if he wants to join Freemasonry for economic advantage, or for any improper purpose. Then he is asked if he will affirm his faith in a Supreme Being. If he answers those questions correctly, he proceeds to the next stage of the Degree.

The Circumambulation. This is just an arcane Masonic term for circling someone, or something. In this stage of the Degree, the Candidate—still blind folded—is led by his Guide around the body of the open lodge three times. He does not know where he is going and must trust his Guide. He is actually circling the Altar and stopping at the stations of the three senior officers of the lodge. Each time around he is stopped by one of them and asked why he has come here, and what is his business? His Guide replies that he has come to seek "Masonic Light" and wisdom.

After giving the password, they proceed on. No lodge room is very big, yet I have known Brethren who swear they walked hundreds of yards during this part of the ceremony. It just seems that way to the uninitiated.

Finally, he is told to stop. He is told to face the East, and take a step forward—the step of an Entered Apprentice Mason. Then he kneels and his hands are placed around something. Since he is still hoodwinked, his actions are narrated for him. He is kneeling at the Altar. The object that he places his hands around, is a book: The Holy Bible, with the Square and Compasses upon it. He is told that the oath he is about to take is old, and is used for tradition's sake. Nothing in it is harmful, or against the laws of his country, state, or religion. The penalties mentioned in the oath are symbolic only and are not to be taken literally.

The Obligation. This word is derived from the Latin *obligare*, "to bind." Specifically, it is called the Oath and Obligation since it consists of particular undertakings (obligations), as well as penalties (the oath), if one breaks one's word. The obligation part deals with secrecy of all kinds. One is to keep much of what one does and experiences as a Freemason secret and inviolate from the outside, "profane," world.*

The obvious question that might occur at this point concerns the entire nature of the book you are now reading. What about the author's Masonic Oath and Obligation? Does everything I've written break my solemn vows? The answer to this question is not a simple one. Like many things in life, the answer is: "it depends."

In some jurisdictions around the nation all writing or communications of any kind dealing with any Masonic information are considered a violation of one's oath. Many jurisdictions even forbid discussing Masonic matters on internet sites under penalty of expulsion from the Brotherhood! No public statements of any kind are permitted without the permission of the proper Masonic authorities. It could be argued (by myself and others) that such rigid discipline is detrimental to Masonry's best interests. Remember that it was born in an era that encouraged freedom of thought and spiritual development. It has always had its roots in The Enlightenment. As a writer I am fortunate to belong to a Grand Lodge that encourages freedom of expression.

Let us continue with the ceremony. The Entered Apprentice is sworn to secrecy and promises to use discretion when talking about Masonic matters. He swears his oath and binds himself with traditional, horrible penalties, calling down vengeance from heaven if he should break his word. He agrees that if he breaks his promise he deserves to be killed, mutilated horribly, and buried in unconsecrated ground. Remember that before the oath was administered, he was told that these penalties are not to be taken literally. They are traditional and are meant to impress upon everyone the solemnity of the promises just made. After this part of the ceremony, the Candidate swears "so help me God," and kisses the Holy Bible to additionally seal his promise.*

Then comes the most memorable part of the initiation ceremony. After once more praying to be brought to "Masonic Light," the Candidate's blindfold is suddenly removed, and the lights are turned on in the lodge room. He kneels there, blinking, blinded, and confused.

Gradually his sight is restored and he is able to make out the Altar, the Holy Bible, the Square and Compasses, and the entire lodge and its officers standing in solemn stillness. He has become an Entered Apprentice Mason. Along with his blindfold, the cable tow is removed from his neck. He can now be trusted symbolically to govern himself without coercion.

The Recapitulation. The name for this part of the

ceremony is self-explanatory: it is a recap, or repetition of the lessons learned. The Candidate—now addressed as "Brother" since he has now become a Mason—receives a lecture from the conferring officer detailing the reasons for the ceremony he has undergone. The petitioning system is narrated and explained. Voting procedures in the lodge are revealed to him. It is emphasized that Freemasonry is an exclusive honor and that high personal standards are expected of the new member. The reason he is wearing only one slipper is explained. It is supposed to commemorate an ancient custom in Israel when promises were exchanged and solemn oaths taken.*

After the lecture is over, the conferring officer* approaches the new Brother and teaches him the step, sign, password, and the handshake of an Entered Apprentice Mason. He tells him the history of the step and sign and what they are named for. Finally, the procedures for entering and leaving an open lodge meeting are outlined. He then directs the new Brother to go with his Guide back to the Preparation Room, where he will change into his normal clothes, and then reenter the lodge room for further instruction and ceremony.

The common gavel and the 24 inch gauge.

The Investiture. After returning from the Preparation room, the new Brother is led by his Guide to the East side of the lodge room where he is met by the Worshipful Master, who invests him with his Masonic apron. He is taught how to wear it as an Entered Apprentice. He is told that it is one of the most ancient of symbols and that nothing is more honorable than for a man to have the right to wear it proudly.

He is told about the significance of the working tools of an Entered Apprentice: the common gavel, and the twenty-four inch gauge. The twenty-four inch gauge is to remind us that there are only twenty-four hours in a day and they must be used wisely. We owe duties to God, to our fellow man, and to ourselves—especially our families. We must try to balance all of those duties.

The common gavel is used by masons to trim stones so that they can be used in a building. We are reminded that we should be polishing our own souls and characters. We are not individuals only; we are part of something bigger and far more important. The Great Achitect created us for a purpose, and that purpose involves working with others and creating something larger than ourselves.

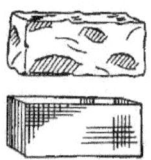

A rough stone and a polished stone. They are emblematic of the work that each individual needs to engage in to improve himself both morally and spiritually.

The Charge. We now come to the final stage of this degree. Still standing before the Worshipful Master, the new Entered Apprentice is given one final lecture in which he is instructed and charged with meeting certain responsibilities as a Mason.

He is reminded of the ancient and honorable history of Freemasonry and that he is expected to conform to its noble ideals. Some of the world's greatest men did not find it beneath their dignity to join the Fraternity and "level" themselves with their brethren and "act upon the square."

He is told that all monotheistic religions are welcome within the lodge and that religious disputes will not be tolerated. The Great Architect of the Universe does not care what church you belong to, he cares about your heart, and your actions here on earth.

As a citizen, a Freemason is to be a loyal and peaceable member of society. He is to engage in charity and benevolence and not be content with doing nothing while there is suffering he can remedy.

He is to behave as a gentleman in the lodge—in the complete sense of that term. He is to treat our ceremonies with the respect that is due them. He is never to mar the harmony and good order of his lodge through jealousy, or a lack of seriousness.

He is to obey the elected and appointed officers of his lodge. He is not to engage in quarrels with critics and enemies of Masonry. He is to improve himself morally and intellectually. He is to conduct his life in such a way that people will ask: "What motivates that man? What is his secret?"

Finally, he is never to recommend a man to become a Freemason unless he truly believes he is able to meet the moral and spiritual requirements of the Brotherhood.

After this short lecture, the new Entered Apprentice is welcomed to the lodge, signs the membership book, and is seated with the Brethren on the "sidelines" (the general seating on the north and south sides of the lodge room).

Such then, is the First Degree, the Entered Apprentice Mason's Degree. When one takes this degree, one is said to have been "Entered."

Pillars & Globes: Earlier in this work, the Temple of Solomon at Jerusalem was mentioned. It had two large pillars at its entrance. These have become an important part of Masonic symbolism. Many lodges have pillars in the West where new members enter the lodge room for the first time. They are usually surmounted by globes. One is the terrestrial, the other the celestial. The terrestrial is more commonly called the earth. The celestial is meant to represent the heavens. They are symbolic of the universality of Freemasonry. Like their originals, the pillars are named Boaz and Jachin. The two pillars also represent the establishment of Strength and rectitude.

THE SECOND DEGREE

In general, one month must pass before a Candidate is eligible to take his Second Degree. There are several reasons for this. First, lodge meetings when degrees are conferred are usually held once a month, so it would be uncommon for a lodge to give two degrees. Second, there are proficiency requirements that must be met before a Brother can receive another degree. These can be quite elaborate and demanding. Finally, Masonic custom recommends a period of reflection as a means of helping each man absorb the lessons of the Craft. A month intuitively feels like the right amount of time.

The proficiency requirements in many Grand Lodge jurisdictions can be strict. Candidates must have memorized the Oath and Obligation. The sign, password, grip, handshake, and working tools must be thoroughly familiar to the new Apprentice. In addition, there are a series of questions and answers about the degree, the symbolism within it, and the actions during the conferral that must be memorized. In many jurisdictions, this process is known as the "catechism." Everything must be memorized word-for-word. New Masons are assigned an instructor who leads him step-by-step through the process. All learning must be done through oral repetition. Nothing can be written down. This is still a good method, and I recommend it. One gets to know one's instructor very well after a month of working and learning with him. This, in turn, helps one to begin meeting the other members of the lodge, and provides a path to becoming an active member.

In many ways, the Second—the Fellow Craft Degree—is my favorite ceremony. The degree, in certain ways, is the "middle child" of the Masonic ritual. It is the shortest of the three degrees. It's the easiest to learn and therefore, the easiest to forget. It is usually treated as an afterthought, even by the Candidate. The First Degree is full of mystery and is the beginning of one's Masonic journey. The Third, or Master Mason's Degree, is the culmination of one's experience in joining the Fraternity. It is the most elaborate of the rituals. The Fellow Craft Degree is usually remembered as just a bridge between the two more memorable ceremonies.

What I like about the Fellow Craft ceremony is that it is more relaxed. The Candidate generally knows what to expect. He knows the form of a degree. He has already experienced what it is like to enter and participate in, a lodge ritual. The nervousness is gone. He can actually relax a little, try to remember his experience, and understand the evening. Like the other degrees, the Fellow Craft is composed of the same basic parts: the preparation, circumambulation, obligation, recapitulation, investiture, and charge.

The Preparation. This part of the degree process takes little time. The Candidate knows exactly where the Preparation Room is, and he knows much more about what is expected of him. He is usually more comfortable with his Guide and everything goes much more smoothly. Physically and spiritually, he is better prepared than before.

With the help of his Guide, he again removes his clothing and dons his special Candidate's garment. This time, however, his right pant leg is rolled up to expose his right knee. He is again barefoot, but a slipper is now worn on his left foot. As before, he has no metal objects or any valuables on his person. The cable tow is now wound twice around his upper left arm. It is used to tie him to his Guide, but he doesn't need to be "forcefully restrained," since he is already knowledgeable about some of the mysteries of the

Craft. When dressed, the Candidate waits with his Guide until the lodge is ready to receive him. He already knows the reasons for his waiting, for his dress, and why he has to wait.

When the proper time comes, the Candidate knocks on the door again. His Guide still speaks for him when the officer enters and enquires about the purpose of his knock. He announces that the Candidate has progressed in his study of the mysteries of Freemasonry, and that he desires to be passed to the Degree of Fellow Craft. After more ceremony and inquiries, as well as giving the password, the Candidate is led into the lodge room.

The Circumambulation. When the Candidate enters the lodge room his movements are similar as in the previous degree. Led by his guide he circles the Altar twice, and stops two times. He is asked by the two senior officers of the lodge what his business is this night. His Guide replies again that he seeks more "Masonic Light," and wisdom. He also wishes to be passed to the Degree of Fellow Craft Mason. In both instances, his Guide must give the password for him to proceed. Finally he is stopped beside the Altar, told to face the East and advance *two* steps this time, where he kneels before the Holy Bible, Square and Compasses.

The Obligation. This next part is also very similar to what was experienced in the previous Degree. In this particular obligation the Candidate repeats much of what he has already promised concerning secrecy. He then makes an additional promise of obedience. He agrees to obey the commands of the lodge, of the officers appointed and elected over him, and also Masonic requests by his fellow Brethren.

As in the First Degree, the oath is sealed with traditional, horrible penalties. He agrees once more that he should die and be horribly mutilated if he breaks his word. Again, before the new Fellow Craft recites his Oath and Obligation, he is reminded by the Worshipful Master that the penalties are traditional only, and are not actually enforced. They are symbolic and are metaphors for invoking punishment from heaven if he should prove a liar and break his word. Just as before, the Candidate swears "so help me God," and kisses the Holy Bible—twice this time—to additionally seal himself to the Brotherhood.

The Recapitulation. This part of the ritual is, again, much shorter than in the previous Degree. The Candidate already understands much that had to be explained before. There is no need to tell him why he wears a special outfit, or one slipper, or why he must not take metal objects into the lodge room. It is, however, repeated that he has bound himself to secrecy and now also to obedience.

The self-developmental aspect of Freemasonry is also emphasized to him. He is enjoined to be a lover of the arts and sciences and to educate himself in the Seven Liberal Arts. Traditionally, they were divided into grammar, rhetoric, logic, arithmetic, geometry, music, and astronomy.* In Masonic symbolism, light is a metaphor for truth and knowledge. All the rituals and ceremonies revolve around seeking differing forms of light. For life to be valuable and rich, we must understand ourselves, our world, the forces of nature, and also the history of mankind. Wisdom is what a man should aspire to, not in order to pose as a learned individual, but in order that he may live a happy and fulfilled life*

The Seven Liberal Arts were so named because the Romans believed they encompassed the proper course of study for a "free" man. Other studies, involving the learning of skills or trades, were for professional purposes. They enabled a man to earn a living. The Liberal Arts gave him a *reason* and *purpose* for living.

Does this mean that Masons are all busy taking extension courses at the local college? Are they required to read a book every week? Of course not. Modern life has to be balanced, and not everyone has the time, or the inclination, to become an amateur academic. What this *does* mean however, is that every Freemason has a responsibility to grow intellectually in some way on a regular basis. All Brethren are aware of their Oath and try to fulfill their obligation.

Finally, the Candidate is shown the step, sign, grip, and handshake of a Fellow Craft Mason. He is also given the password. Their origin and significance are explained. He is told how to enter, and leave, a lodge of Fellow Craft Masons. As before, he is sent out of the lodge room to change into his original clothing and return for further instruction.

The Investiture. Again, as in the previous degree, the new Fellow Craft is led by his Guide to the East side of the lodge. He is met by the Worshipful Master who invests him with his Masonic apron. He is taught how to wear it in the fashion of a Fellow Craft Mason. He has already been taught about the significance of the apron from the previous lecture.

Next, the working tools of a Fellow Craft Mason are explained to him. They are: the plumb, the level, and the square. The plumb is a tool used by actual masons to make sure that perpendicular lines are correct.

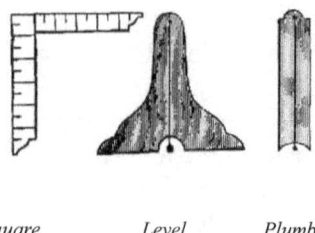

Square   *Level*   *Plumb*

The level is used to make sure that horizontals are in alignment. The square is to make sure that corners are truly at 90 degree angles. These tools are obviously of value when building a structure. He is shown that these tools remind Freemasons to be proud and upright in their lives, doing good to all. A brother should meet his fellows "on the square," treating everyone he meets with honesty and justice. Finally, he is reminded that all of us are making a journey on the level of time. That journey will end someday, and when we reach our destination, we will have to answer for our actions during this life.

Doric   *Corinthian*

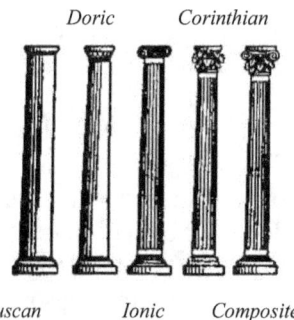

Tuscan   *Ionic*   *Composite*

Next, the Candidate is instructed concerning the five classical orders of architecture: the Tuscan, Doric, Ionic, Corinthian, and Composite. These orders were invented by the ancient Greeks and Romans. The Tuscan is the plainest, least adorned order, the Composite the most elaborate. Each was used to build a unified, symetrical structure. If you look around, you can easily see their influence to this day on our buildings. Freemasons are still builders, but we expend our energy building a spiritual temple; our character, our soul. Choose wisely when constructing your spiritual self. Don't just use odds and ends that come to hand. Have a plan and carry it through. As each order of architecture has a unified conception, so should your individual life plan.*

Just as architecture was at one time seen as the search for order amidst chaos, so the Freemason should seek order in his life, in his spirit, and in his intellectual development.

The letter "G" is a symbol that is commonly associated with Freemasonry. It is said by many to stand for geometry, which originally was synonymous with masonry. It also has a religious significance. It, of course

G

stands for GOD and should always remind the Freemason that we are dependent upon the Creator in all things. We should remember to place our faith and trust in The Great Architect of the Universe. Every time he sees the Masonic symbol, and what is at its center, this lesson should be reinforced in his mind.

The Charge. We now come to the final stage in the degree. The new Fellow Craft is given a final lecture by the Master in which he is instructed and charged with meeting additional responsibilities as is expected of a Mason who has been passed to a higher degree.

First, he is congratulated on his advancement in Freemasonry. He is reminded that he is still being judged upon his character and qualifications to fully enter into the Brotherhood. He has met the tests so far, and has, therefore, merited the additional honor of this Degree.

Next, he is again advised to improve himself by polishing his mind and character through the study of the Liberal Arts. Geometry, and its implications for order and design, are earnestly recommended to him. Just as a building depends upon the principles of geometry to stand upright, so a man's character and soul depend on an intelligent design to develop to the fullest. Also, just as a building cannot exist without an architect, so the world is the product of the One Great Architect. He is requested to always remember this fact.

Thirdly, the new Fellow Craft is again warned that he must live up to the standards expected of a Freemason. He is to attend lodge faithfully, to treat its ceremonies and customs with respect and veneration, and induce others to do the same.

Finally, he is reminded of his oath of obedience which has formed such a large section of the Second Degree. He is to obey all requests and summons from his lodge, and from his fellow Masons, when duly received from the proper Masonic authority.

THE THIRD DEGREE

The Third Degree is officially known as the

Sublime Degree of Master Mason. It is the highest Degree, and the highest honor, that a Freemason can achieve. There are many other Masonic groups and bodies that give degrees with larger numbers—the most notable being the Scottish Rites' 32nd Degree. Many outsiders (the *profane*), mistakenly believe that these degrees are somehow superior, and that being awarded them makes one a more "important" Mason. This is a misconception. These other bodies are important, but after receiving the Sublime Degree of Master Mason, a member has achieved the pinnacle in Freemasonry. We will cover these other "Appendant" groups in another chapter.

After the customary period of one month, during which time knowledge proficiency is demonstrated by the new Fellow Craft, the Master Mason's Degree is ready to be conferred. By this time, the Candidate has a very good idea of what will happen to him, and how he is to be prepared for the ritual. At this point in the initiation rituals, a final series of revelations are revealed. As in other areas of life, just when you think you know it all, surprises spring up.

The Third Degree is much more elaborate than the first two. It is the longest degree, sometimes taking several hours to complete. It has another section to it that the other Degrees do not have. It also explains some puzzles from the two previous ceremonies. Words, actions, and phrases that were obscure until this point are illuminated in this Degree. Finally, the entire purpose and meaning, as well as the legend of the birth of the Brotherhood, are disclosed. It's a memorable evening for the Candidate.

The Preparation. As in the Fellow Craft Degree, the Candidate arrives relaxed and confident. He feels that he knows what will happen and is usually looking forward to finishing his Masonic journey and becoming a full-fledged Freemason. As soon as he enters the Preparing Room, however, things start to take a slightly unexpected turn. After removing his clothes and his personal possessions, he finds that his Candidate's costume is significantly different than before. It now consists only of the trousers. He is bare-chested. Both of his pant legs are rolled up so that his knees are bare. No slippers are worn. He is barefoot. The cable tow is now wound three times around his waist. Already cold, and a little embarrassed, he knocks on the door to the lodge three times and lets his Guide answer the now familiar questions as to his purpose this night.

The Circumambulation. When he enters the body of the open lodge, he is led by his Guide once around the Altar, stopping in front of the Worshipful Master who asks why he has come here? His Guide replies that he seeks still more "Masonic Light" and wisdom. He wishes to be further instructed in the mysteries of Freemasonry and be raised to the Sublime Degree of Master Mason. His Guide gives the proper password. Then he is taken to the Altar, told to face the East and take *three* steps. He kneels before the Altar, lays his hands upon the Holy Bible, Square, and Compasses, and takes the Oath and Obligation of a Master Mason.

The Obligation. In this particular obligation the Candidate again repeats much of what he has already promised concerning secrecy and obedience. He also agrees to perform many other additional duties. It is the longest of the three obligations by far. He agrees to support and obey the rules and regulations of his lodge and also of the Grand Lodge. He agrees to support and defend all

Brother Master Masons. He also promises to be charitable to all people, but especially to fellow Brethren. He agrees to uphold the Masonic traditions of morality, good character, belief in a Creator, and also swears to follow the traditional Masonic rules against letting underage men, those of unsound mind, or women, join the Fraternity.

As in the other Degrees, the oath is sealed with traditional, horrible penalties. He agrees that his body should be torn apart, burned, and the ashes scattered, if he breaks his word. Again, before promising this, he is reminded by the Worshipful Master that the penalties are allegorical only and are not ever enforced. And finally, just as is the previous Degrees, the Candidate swears "so help me God," and kisses the Holy Bible—three times this time—to additionally seal himself to the Brotherhood.

The Recapitulation. This part is also very similar to the previous Degrees. The Worshipful Master goes over the entire ceremony up to that point and explains the significance of the actions the Candidate was instructed to perform. For example, his bare feet are intended to remind him of the story of Moses and the burning bush. God commanded Moses to remove his sandals in his presence.* The reason he entered the lodge room shirtless, was to prove that he was not a woman, for only males are allowed to join the Fraternity.

After these preliminaries, the Worshipful Master shows the step, sign, password, and gives the handshake of a Master Mason. Their origin and significance are explained. The Candidate is also told how to enter and leave a lodge of Master Masons. At this point, however, the Degree changes. Instead of returning to the Preparing Room and changing into his regular clothes, the Worshipful Master does not let go of the Candidate's hand. Instead, he conducts him to the East, directly in front of the station of the Master, at the foot of the three steps of the raised platform.

Lecture in the East. It is now that the Candidate suddenly realizes that the ritual has changed radically and this will not be the familiar experience that he has gone through before. Still standing half-naked in the East, he is now the sole recipient of an oration by the Master which details the origins of the Craft.

The lecture deals with the legend of the death of Hiram Abiff and the building of the Temple at Jerusalem by King Solomon. It is unclear when this story entered Masonic lore. The first published reference to it is contained in James Anderson's 1723 work, *The Constitutions of the Free-Masons.** The allusion is fairly cryptic however. Only much later in the 1700's did the tale become a basic element within the ritual.*

The skeleton of the story is found in the Holy Bible in I Kings, 6-8, and in II Chronicles, 2-7. King David, after unifying the Hebrew tribes and creating the Kingdom of Israel, wished to crown his reign by building a temple to Jehovah in the city of Jerusalem. For a variety of reasons, he could not accomplish this aim and contented himself with gathering materials for the project. He left it to his son and successor King Solomon to carry out his ambition. Solomon realized that his small country lacked the necessary architects and builders, so he asked an ally, King Hiram of Tyre for help. Hiram gladly supplied materials and also expert planners and craftsmen. One of these builders was named Hiram Abiff.* With the help of this master craftsman, and other aid supplied by the Tyrians, the Temple at Jerusalem was completed and dedicated by King Solomon. Such is the story found in the Holy Bible.

Masonic lore contains additional elements not found within the biblical record. According to this version, King Solomon of Israel, King Hiram of Tyre, and Hiram Abiff jointly planned and built the temple. They each took the title of "Grand Master" and presided over the thousands of masters, fellow crafts, and apprentices while the temple construction was proceeding.

When the project was almost finished, the three Grand Masters decided that the most worthy of the fellow crafts would be promoted to the status of master so that they could travel about the world and earn their livings on their own. In order to prove their credentials, they would be given the secret password, sign, and handshake of a master mason. These honors could only be given by the three Grand Masters together, since they had sworn an oath to heaven to only reveal the words and signs jointly.

Word of the promotions soon leaked out among the workmen. Fifteen fellow crafts decided to steal the credentials of a master, since they did not feel they would merit them on their own. Twelve lost their nerve but three decided to carry out their plan. They ambushed Hiram Abiff one morning as he was leaving the temple where he conducted morning devotions alone before planning the day's work. They stationed themselves at the east, west, and southern gates of the temple and demanded the word and sign of a master. Hiram refused three times, and after being attacked by each fellow craft in turn, was finally killed by the last with a blow to the head from a setting maul.

A representation of a setting maul.

The three fellow crafts then buried his body and fled in shame and terror over their deed. The next day, the crime was revealed, and the plot uncovered by King Solomon and King Hiram. Aside from the horror of the murder itself, the two Grand Masters realized that the secret word and sign of a master mason was lost forever. The three of them had sworn to confer it jointly, and since one of them was dead, they now could never reveal it to anyone. The twelve fellow crafts who had lost their nerve confessed and were sent to find the three murderers. They were found and speedily brought back before King Solomon, who passed judgment upon them. Later, the twelve were sent to find the location where the body of Hiram Abiff was buried and hidden.

The corpse was eventually found because the murderers had marked the grave with a sprig of acacia. It was dug up and the first words spoken were adopted as the secret word of a Master Mason. Likewise, the hand clasp used to pull the body out of its grave became the grip of a Master Mason.

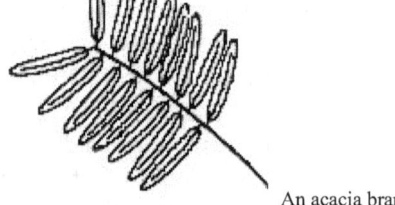

An acacia branch.

As the lecture proceeds to the story of Hiram Abiff's murder, the Candidate's role changes from listener to participant in the ritual. As the story of the murder in the temple is outlined, the Candidate is led around the lodge floor and realizes that he is now standing in for the murdered master. He is also symbolically buried and then found. It is a powerful experience. This part of the ceremony ends with the Candidate receiving the Adopted Secret Word of a Master Mason and the accompanying grip. After this part of the ritual, the Candidate is sent back to the preparation room with his Guide in order to change back into his own clothes. As before, there are two more very important parts of the ceremony left.

The Investiture. As in the previous Degrees, the new Master Mason is led by his Guide to the east end of the lodge room. He now climbs to the third step of the platform there, and is met by the Worshipful Master who invests him with his Masonic apron. He is taught how to wear it in the proper fashion of a Master Mason.

He is told that the working tools of a Master Mason are all of the ones from the previous degrees. There is a new one however, the trowel. He is reminded that, as real workmen use the trowel to spread cement, Freemasons use the trowel to remind themselves to spread brotherly love and affection among each other, and among mankind in general.

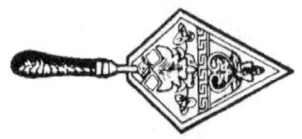

Next, the duty of helping others, especially fellow Freemasons, is stressed. Antique signs of distress, and their accompanying code words are given to the new member of the lodge. He is reminded that he has a duty as a

Freemason, and as a human being, to help everyone as much as he can.

The Charge. We now come to the final stage in the Degree. The new Master Mason is congratulated on his latest achievement. He is now a full-fledged member of the Fraternity. He has no more tests to meet, no more rituals to undergo. He has arrived. He is reminded however, of the additional promises he has made during this Degree. All the previous agreements promising obedience and secrecy still are in force. Additionally, the new Freemason is charged with helping his Brethren if they should fall into error. He is also reminded to uphold the traditions and laws of his individual lodge, the Grand Lodge of Pennsylvania, and of any other Masonic organization under whose authority he may find himself.

He is reminded that he is now a full member of his lodge. He is now privileged to speak, to vote, and to propose other men for membership in the Fraternity. He is to always remember the sacred trust that has been placed in him by his Brethren. He is to conduct himself always as a gentleman and to remember that he represents Freemasonry wherever he goes. He is to help all people, but especially fellow Freemasons, and is never to knowingly hurt a Brother in any way. Finally, he is congratulated once more, shakes hands with the Master, and takes his seat with the rest of the Brethren.

In many lodges there are additional customs and ceremonies at this point. Often a Masonic lapel pin is presented to the new Mason, or sometimes a relative or friend will give him a ring. Sometimes the new Brother is presented with the Bible that was used in all of his Degrees. There are pages inside for his name, the dates of his Degrees, and the names of the conferring officers. There is also space for all of the attendees to sign. The Brother who signed his application and recommended him for membership normally buys this gift. After additional greetings and congratulations, the newly raised Brother is asked to say a few words. Afterwards, the lodge adjourns for a meal together.

In some jurisdictions there are additional sections to this final Degree. After dinner, there may be more lectures on the history of the Craft, often accompanied by slide shows and other entertainments. Often these other elements to the evening take up an additional hour, making it a long evening for the new Mason.

Such then, is the Third Degree, the Sublime Degree of Master Mason. I must emphasize that this is the basic form of the ceremony. Many unimportant details have been omitted. Also, remember that just as there is no centralized Masonic leadership in North America, there is no standard ritual as well. If one were to travel from state to state, or into Canada (and were a member of the Fraternity), a great variety of customs and variations would be evident. Still and all, what has been presented in this chapter should satisfy the curious and answer serious questions about "what goes on inside those Masonic buildings."

The Square and Compasses with the letter G. The best known symbols of Freemasonry. The square is meant to remind the individual to square his actions by the square of virtue. The Compasses are to remind him to circumscribe his desires and to keep them within due bounds. The G stands for geometry, but should also remind the Freemason of God and the creator's place in his life.

Reports

     Near the end of any lodge meeting the sometimes mundane part of the evening must be addressed. Reports of standing committees in the lodge are given. These can range from charity committees, youth groups, to visitation of sick Brethren. One of the most important reports is from the Treasurer.

     The Crossed Keys are the symbol of the Lodge Treasurer. He wears a small version of them around his neck as his jewel of office. He is responsible for keeping the financial books of the Lodge in order. He originates payments, receives dues, and must be one of the officers that signs all checks. It is a big responsibility and normally is filled by a Past Master. Election is usually of one year, but good Treasurers are often reelected.

EMBLEMATIC STRUCTURE OF FREEMASONRY

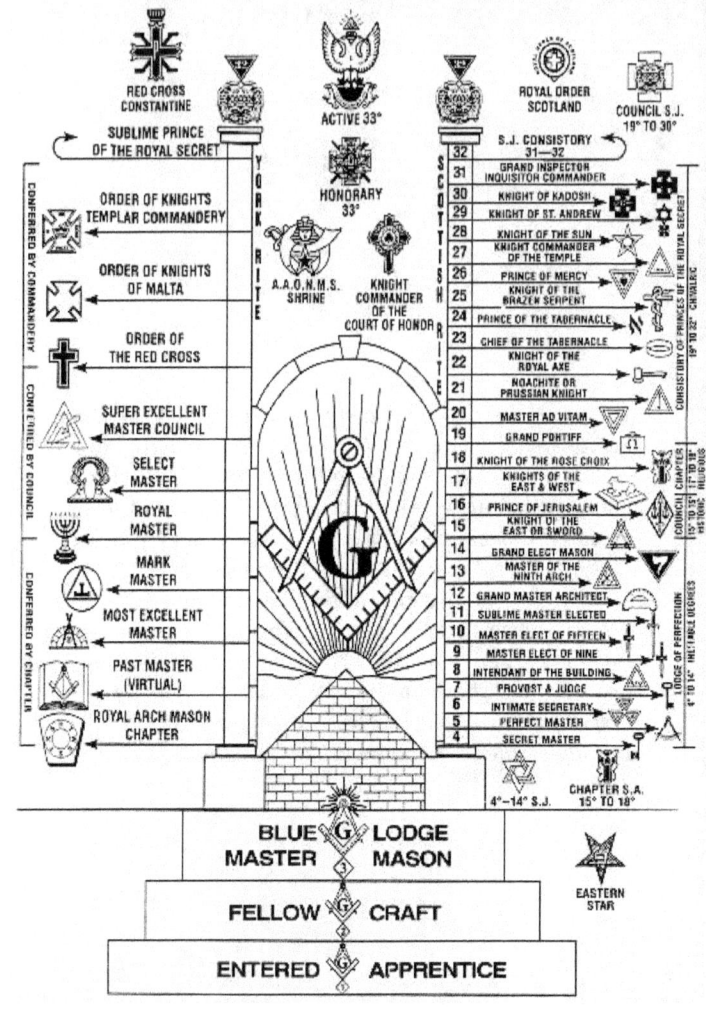

APPENDANT BODIES

We have outlined some of the history of the Fraternity, covered the structure of a "typical" lodge and its officers, and given an overview of the three basic degrees. So far Freemasonry has seemed orderly and easy to understand. Simplicity ends at this juncture. The Fraternity has many other options to experience and other Masonic bodies to join. They are called the "Appendant Orders." The word commonly means "attached" although these groups are mostly self-governing. The Shrine, for example, is independent of other Masonic bodies. There are so many of these additional groups that a chart is necessary in order to understand their relationship. Look on the previous page and you will see what I mean. It looks confusing, but bear with me. There is a logic to the system.

Basic Masonic membership is sometime referred to as "Blue Lodge," or "Craft" Masonry. The reason for this is that each body has a dominant color associated with it. Light blue, or sky blue, has always been a motif in lodges. Craft Masonry forms the foundation for the Appendant Orders. Only Master Masons in good standing are eligible for membership in most of these other branches of the Craft. There are two major bodies: "The York Rite," and "The Scottish Rite."

On the left of the diagram is the older branch: "The York Rite." On the right is "The Scottish Rite." The York Rite grew out of Eighteenth Century Freemasonry. In fact, one of its Degrees, The Royal Arch, was conferred as early as the 1750's in America. The Scottish Rite originated in France in the latter half of the 1700's and came to the United States in 1801. Both of these bodies are old and distinguished organizations. They both offer significant opportunities, but they are different in style, and in how they are organized.

Each confers degrees in a different manner, and each offers a different experience to its members. Don't get the idea however, that one is in any way superior to the other, or to basic Masonic lodge membership. In fact, if for any reason a Freemason chooses to resign from his "Blue Lodge," he automatically loses his memberships in any other Masonic body that he may have joined. The degree of Master Mason is the most important title that any Freemason can receive.

THE SCOTTISH RITE

We will begin with the Scottish Rite on the right hand side the chart. This has long been a popular Appendant body. It is probably one of the best known to the general public of the Masonic bodies. It has an expansive list of degrees that it confers, the last one being the 32nd Degree. The Scottish Rite is organized in a much different manner than basic "Craft" Masonry. It does not meet locally in lodges, but in a much larger body called a "Valley." These Valleys cover wide areas and draw members from surrounding towns and municipalities. Instead of meeting in individual Masonic Temples, they use large buildings called "Scottish Rite Cathedrals." Instead of monthly, Degrees are conferred a few times a year during special meetings called "Reunions."

The structure of the Degrees is much different than in the "Blue Lodge." To begin with, there are usually dozens of Candidates for the Scottish Rite, sometimes a hundred men or more. Reunions only last a few days, so the ritual work must, of necessity, be on a mass scale. The Degrees are conferred in a Cathedral's auditorium and all the Candidates sit in the audience and watch the Degree performed onstage by a cast of characters. Next, one individual Candidate is selected from the group to "exemplify," or represent, all the other applicants. Degrees are presented in the form of plays, with dialogue and costumes. Some are very elaborate. Finally, since each ceremony lasts an hour or more, there is not enough time to present all 32 Degrees to a group of new members. About six or so are presented over the course of the two-day reunion.

The Degrees can be very entertaining and thought provoking, but individual participation must, of course be kept to a minimum. Scottish Rite Cathedrals are very social in their orientation. They are more welcoming to the individual member's families and the community. They sponsor dinners, civic entertainments, picnics, and outings.

The symbol of the Scottish Rite: the double-headed eagle. It was adopted in the early 1800's from an old Crusader symbol, although the use of the eagle as an emblem is very old. The number "32" refers to the highest earned degree that the Rite confers. The crest is a common one seen on many Masonic rings.

The Scottish Rite is a fine organization but has been misunderstood by the general public due to the numbering of its degrees. Many mistakenly believe that if one joins the Rite, that one is a "higher ranking" Freemason than a Master Mason who has received the 3rd Degree. This is understandable, but let me emphasize once again that the Scottish Rite is simply an additional Masonic body that a Freemason may join. Membership confers no advantage, or additional rank within the Fraternity.

There is one more degree that the Scottish Rite confers: the 33rd. It is an honorific bestowed for service to the Fraternity and for civic achievement. There are two types, active and honorary. An active 33rd is given to the elected leaders of the Scottish Rite. An Inactive (or honorary) 33rd is awarded to those members who have contributed long and honorable service to the Rite, or who have outstanding citizens.

THE YORK RITE

Chapter   *Council*   *Commandery*

Next comes the York Rite of Freemasonry (on the left side of the chart). The York Rite is best understood as a continuation of the degrees conferred in the Masonic lodge. There are three bodies within the Rite: the Royal Arch Chapter, the Council of Royal and Select Master Masons, and the Commandery of Knights Templar. A Candidate may join only one body, but normally he joins all three. It can take up to a year to progress through all the Degrees. Chapter and Council Degrees build on the Biblical story of the Temple of Solomon at Jerusalem and its eventual destruction by the Babylonians. It continues the story through the restoration of the temple and the rebuilding of the city of Jerusalem. The Commandery is based on the historical warrior monks, the Knights Templar. It is also one of the few bodies within Freemasonry that is strongly religious in character and only accepts Candidates who profess a belief in Christianity. It is, therefore, an exception to the rule of keeping religious differences out of Masonry. The Degrees are much like the ones conferred in the Blue Lodge. Usually there is only one Candidate, and he is the focus of the evening. York Rite bodies meet once a month in a fashion similar to Masonic lodges. They have their own officers and Degree nights. The ritualistic work of the three bodies would look somewhat familiar to a Master Mason and so would the Degrees for the most part. There are nine degrees in York Rite Masonry, although no one goes around speaking of himself as a "Ninth Degree" York Mason.

THE RED CROSS OF CONSTANTINE

The Red Cross of Constantine is an additional order of knighthood open to members of the York Rite. It is also overtly religious in character as applicants must profess a belief in Christianity. The order confers a degree based upon the story of the Emperor Constantine, his conversion to Christianity, and the Battle of the Milvian Bridge. Members are referred to as "Knight Masons," and meet in lodge-like settings known as Conclaves.

SHRINERS INTERNATIONAL

The Shrine has the biggest public profile of all the additional Masonic bodies. They host the Shrine Circuses in cities all over America, they march in parades and most importantly, they own the twenty-two Shriners Hospitals for Children. The organization is even larger than the Scottish Rite. They are organized into "Mosques" and draw members from even larger areas around them. Normally there are only a few in an entire state. In order to join the Shrine, one must be a Master Mason in good standing at one's local lodge. There are no additional qualifications. In addition, the Shrine is self-governing, has a national leadership, and in not dependent on any Grand Lodge for its authority.

The Shrine is dedicated to good works and helping children, but the organization is also devoted to fun, and good fellowship. There are dinners, clubs, groups of all kinds to join, and family activities are stressed. The

initiation is given *en mass* as in the Scottish Rite at a
a "Ceremonial," usually held twice a year. It also resembles
attending a play and there is one Candidate onstage who
stands in for the entire class of entrants.

The Shrine was founded in 1872 by a group of
Freemasons in New York City.* At the time, fascination
with the Middle East was in fashion. Egyptian motifs in
decoration and architecture, curiosity about Islam, and tales
of the Arabian Nights were common. Arabian trappings
such as scimitars, the red fez, and pseudo-eastern names
were adopted to add glamour and mystery to the new group.
To this day, Shrine meetings are held in "Mosques," and
members wear a distinctive red Fez. Once known as the
"Ancient Arabic Order of the Nobles of the Mystic Shrine
(A.A.O.N.M.S)," the name was changed in recent years to
"Shriners International."

For the next fifty years the Shrine lived up to the
nickname one of its founding members had coined: "The
Playground of Masonry." Perhaps it lived up to this concept
too well. By 1920, the public image of this Masonic group
had suffered mightily. A common phrase of the time that
described a drunken, disorderly spectacle was "a Shriner's
Convention."

At the National Imperial Council meeting in
Portland Oregon, Forrest Adair, then head of the Scottish
Rite in Atlanta called on the Shrine to reform its image and
devote some of its energies to philanthropy.*

The result was the system of Shriner's Hospitals
supported by the Fraternity that provides care to children all
over North America and from around the world. It is one of
the most successful charities in existence and has treated
innumerable patients whose families could not pay for
medical care. It is one of the great Masonic achievements of
the Twentieth Century.

OTHER BODIES

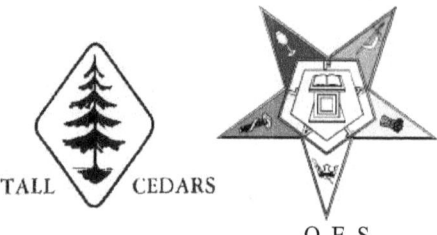

O. E. S.

There are two other Appendant bodies that should be mentioned next: the Grotto, and the Tall Cedars of Lebanon. The formal title of the Grotto is the "Mystic Order of Veiled Prophets of the Enchanted Realm." The organization is smaller than the Shrine but operates in much the same way, being dedicated to fun and good fellowship. Like the Shrine, it has adopted a Middle Eastern flavor in organization and ceremony. Their initiation is somewhat similar as well to the Shrine's. The Tall Cedars of Lebanon is also oriented towards recreation and relaxation. Both of these groups require only that a prospective member be a Master Mason.

The Order of the Eastern Star is unusual within Freemasonry in that it is a co-ed body that men *and* women can join. Indeed, it was invented in the Nineteenth Century in order to give women a chance to experience Masonry in some form. Many husbands and wives join so that they can share the Masonic experience together. A Chapter must be sponsored by a Masonic Lodge, but it is run by its female members, with males as advisors only.

Closing

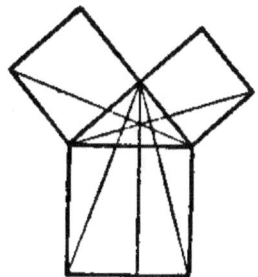

       The Forty-Seventh Problem of Euclid* is one of the most important calculations used in geometry. It proves that the square formed on the hypotenuse of a triangle (the longest side) is equal to the sum of the squares formed on the other, shorter sides. From this seemingly simple formula much of the builder's trade is derived. It is a pervasive symbol in Freemasonry and is the symbol of a Past Master in many jurisdictions.

       Closing a lodge is the final ceremony of a meeting. It is elaborate and stately, and consists of the officers and Brethren preparing to end their time together in Masonic harmony and reenter the everyday, outside, "profane" world. Hopefully, the meeting has strengthened their resolve to practice the Masonic virtues of Faith, Hope, and Charity in their lives.

The apron of a Fellow Craft Mason. It is worn with the upper flap turned down, and the left-hand corner turned up and tucked behind. Tradition has it that this made it easier for the experienced workman to carry his tools around the worksite. It left his hands free. This is how Brethren are taught to wear their aprons in the course of the Second Degree.

CHALLENGES TO FREEMASONRY

Attacks on Freemasonry are actually older than the organization itself—or at least older than the Grand Lodge of England. In 1698 a handbill was circulated in London condemning that "devilish sect of men...evildoers ...corrupt people." It alerted "all godly people in the citie of London" about the "Mischiefs and Evil practiced in the sight of GOD by those called Freed Masons."* This was a full 19 years before the Grand Lodge of England organized itself in 1717! Assaults on Freemasonry have not stopped since. Members have come to expect criticisms of the Fraternity in the media, and even among friends and acquaintances. This chapter is meant to outline the basic criticisms of Masonry and give some basic facts in order to let the reader judge their validity.

Criticisms of the Fraternity fall into three general categories: religious objections, charges of conspiracy, and imputations of racism. We will deal with each in turn. The vast majority of allegations made against Masons are nonsense. Some however, have a basis in fact.

Religious Objections. Given that one of Freemasonry's basic beliefs is freedom of personal conscience in religious matters, it is not surprising that organized religion has historically been an enemy of the Brotherhood. I will begin with the Roman Catholic Church and its position concerning our Order. There are several reasons for starting here. First, it is the largest Christian church in the world. Second, it is the oldest, most powerful, and most prestigious denomination. Lastly, it has the longest record of sustained criticisms of Freemasonry.

Soon after Masonry appeared in Europe, the

Vatican made its first pronouncement against the Fraternity. In 1737, Pope Clement XII issued a Papal Bull forbidding Catholics to become Masons. Since then, eight popes in seventeen different proclamations have condemned Freemasonry and threatened Catholics with the punishment of excommunication for joining the organization.* In 1884, Pope Leo XIII issued *Humanum Genus*, the strongest condemnation of Freemasonry ever issued by the Church, and one that still technically remains in force today.

In this document, Leo outlined the main issues that the Catholic Church has with the Brotherhood. He charged the Masonic Fraternity with conducting a world-wide conspiracy to undermine and attack the Catholic Church. He complained that the Italian unification of 1870 was the result of a Masonic plot. He also charged Freemasons with being guilty of encouraging *indifferentism*—the belief that all religious beliefs are the same and all are equally valid. *Humanum Genus* also accused Freemasons of belief in the following errors: democratic government, separation of church and state, public schooling, and freedom of conscience!*

I believe it likely that most Freemasons would plead guilty to believing in democracy and freedom of religion. The charges of conspiracy are harder to disprove since one would be forced to prove a negative. The facts of history tell us however, that while Garibaldi was a Freemason, the Italian unification movement was not a Masonic plot. Neither Communism nor Fascism were—or are—connected with the Fraternity as well.

Things got even more complicated for Roman Catholic laymen who were interested in joining the lodge. In 1974, the Congregation for the Doctrine of the Faith issued a letter stating that Catholic laymen were permitted to join any organization as long as it did not conspire against the Church.* Freemasonry was specifically *not* mentioned in this document. This was strange since the very question it dealt with concerned Freemasonry. In addition, the official 1994 *Catechism of the Catholic Church* actually *requires* Catholics to "take an active part in public life...participation may vary from one...culture to another."* Then in 1983, the Congregation issued a new letter restating the Church's old position of forbidding any membership in Freemasonry. This muddied the waters even further.

As a member in good standing, I would make the following case for the lodge: first, Freemasonry is not a religion or a religious organization. It teaches no doctrine of salvation or path to God. It assumes that its members believe in a single deity, but it does not ask for a profession of faith. In fact, religious matters are not spoken of inside the lodge. Second, Freemasonry is a secular organization concerned with charity, self-improvement, and patriotism. In today's world, it actively supports the United States of America, and it assuredly does *not* conspire against the Church. Third, Freemasons *do* believe in freedom of conscience, separation of church and state, and public education.

It should not be necessary to apologize for holding these beliefs. To sum up: most of the Church's accusations are either untrue, or are invalid. Freemasons might quote Cardinal John Newman and claim the supremacy of individual conscience over the authority of religious leaders of any church.

The Catholic Church is not alone among Christian denominations who have made attacks on Freemasonry. Evangelical fundamentalist ministers have chosen Masonry as a target in recent decades. Many "televangelists" use

Freemasonry as a whipping boy. Freemasons are accused of taking "false oaths," or of disobeying the biblical injunction to not swear oaths at all. Masons are also actually accused by some of worshiping the devil. Some critics allege that the Lodge has created a religion separate from Christianity. They charge Freemasons with ignoring the Christian doctrine of faith through Jesus Christ, and with preaching salvation through good works alone.

To repeat once again: Freemasonry assumes that one believes in a Supreme Being as a condition of membership. It does not teach a path of salvation and does not recommend any religious course in life. If one wants religious instruction, one should go to a priest, rabbi, minister, or some other religious teacher. Masonry does not have a creed, or a doctrine for gaining eternal life. One should go to a church to find these things.

As to the accusations of devil worship, usually critics will pick out a Masonic writer from the past and selectively quote him as an authority on Freemasonry. Brother Albert Pike is a favorite writer used by these detractors. Pike wrote prolifically in the Nineteenth Century about Masonic topics. Much of what he wrote deals with his personal musings on religion and philosophy. Antagonists will usually start by saying that Pike is "The Authority" on Freemasonry. Then they will quote a few lines in order to "prove" that Freemasons worship Satan. Again, there *is* no authority that speaks for Masonry! Quoting Pike or anyone else does not win an argument!

Personal experience has shown that most of these fundamentalists, if you dig a little, believe that everyone but their own followers are headed for perdition. One such evangelist used to sell a whole series of books, videos, and recordings dealing with religious topics. Once I looked up the list of what was for sale and what "good" Christians should beware of. The list was endless. Freemasons, Catholics, Jews, Muslims, Lutherans, Baptists, Hindus, Mormons, Buddhists—you name it—they were bad. The only group that one could safely belong to was the one headed by the evangelical leader—oh, and don't neglect to send money to him and his "ministry."

Let me close by repeating that Masonic oaths and obligations are symbolic only. The Candidate is told this at every step in the process of joining. They are traditional and serve to reinforce the solemnity of the occasion. Finally, there is nothing wrong with taking an oath, *per se*. Many citizens take them when called for jury duty, when testifying in court, when enlisting in the armed services, or when taking a job in government. Most citizens take these various oaths throughout their lives and don't feel that their souls are in danger. Masonic obligations are no different.

Conspiracy Charges. Believe it or not, there are even more extreme charges than devil worship made against the Fraternity. Some writers claim that Freemasons are part of a world-wide conspiracy that controls finance, governments, and all major institutions. Many writers have made a good living helping to spread this thesis. One of the first, Leo Taxil, published his *Complete Revelation upon Freemasonry* in 1885 in France. This was the first of a series of books in which he claimed to "expose" the perils of the international Masonic conspiracy. He charged that Albert Pike was the "Pope" of the organization, that a congress had been held in Paris to plan world revolution, and that Freemasons practiced free sex and worshiped the devil. He completely fooled Catholic leaders of the time and received handsome payments and honors from the Vatican. It was somewhat embarrassing when he publicly admitted in 1895 that everything he had written was pure fabrication.*

In the 1970's, British journalist Steven Knight published a series of books in which he accused Freemasons in England of dominating the Home Office and the London Police. He also implied that Freemasons had been involved in a cover-up involving the "Jack the Ripper" murder case in the 1890's. Either the perpetrator, the investigating officials, or the Commissioner of the Metropolitan Police Force were Freemasons and had some mysterious interest in leaving the case unsolved.*

There *was* a financial scandal with Masonic overtones in Italy in the 1970's. A Masonic Lodge of Research named *Propaganda Due* or P-2 was expelled by the Italian Grand Lodge and its warrant confiscated. The master of the lodge continued to hold meetings and converted it to his own purposes. He eventually used it to build a network of politicians, bankers, and publishers throughout Italy. Many members of P-2 were implicated in a financial scandal involving banks closely allied to the Vatican. The story is too complex to relate here, but it involved embezzlement, murder, Catholic Church officials, and hundreds of millions of missing dollars. Even though it was really a Vatican scandal, Freemasonry was also tarred with it as well.*

As with many conspiracy theories, one can never marshal enough facts to stay ahead of the charges. The truth simply doesn't matter at a certain point. For example, to this day one can buy a copy of a book entitled *Protocols of the Elders of Zion* which "proves" there is an international Jewish conspiracy controlling the world. The fact that the book was fabricated in 1902 by the Russian Czar's secret police doesn't matter to some people today. With the invention of the internet in the last thirty years, it is literally impossible to combat the errors and conspiracy theories circulating around the globe. This will probably be a permanent problem for Freemasonry in the future.

Racism. Charges that Freemasonry is a racist organization make some of the Brethren squirm since this charge has some basis in historical fact. Remember, Freemasonry can be defined as "The Brotherhood of Man, under the Fatherhood of God." All men who are of good character, believe in a Supreme Being, and can financially bear the burden, are eligible for membership.

However Masonry has usually reflected the individual society in which it exists. For much of the history of the United States formal, and informal, racial segregation has been a fact of life. This carried over into Masonic custom. Most lodges have been overwhelmingly white. This was reflected all across the nation and compelled black men to form separate lodges if they wanted to become Freemasons.

In 1775, an African American named Prince Hall, and fourteen other individuals, were initiated in Irish Military Lodge No. 441 in Boston, Massachusetts. The city was then under occupation by the British Army. Hall formed African Lodge No. 1 by authority given him by this army lodge. This was a normal practice of the day.

When English forces were driven out of Boston in 1776, Hall and his fellows attempted to join re-established (white) lodges in the city. They were rejected (probably for racial reasons). Hall and his Brethren secured a warrant for their lodge from the Grand Lodge of England in 1784. It also gave them the authority to form other lodges, and even grand lodges in North America. This was the Masonic basis for what came to be called "Prince Hall Masonry."

In state after state, black men who wished to join

the Fraternity had to enter the Brotherhood through these competing Grand Lodges. Even though they were lawfully organized under the authority of the English Grand Lodge, they were treated as unlawful, clandestine organizations by the "Regular" (white) Grand Lodges in each state.

In 1813, The Grand Lodge of England reorganized itself into the "United Grand Lodge of England." It also canceled many of the warrants that had been granted previously in years past. One of these warrants was the one for African Lodge No. 1. This eliminated the legitimacy of the lodge since no American Grand Lodge stepped in and recognized its members as Freemasons. In turn, all of the lodges and Grand Lodges across the United States that traced their warrants to it were, in turn, now considered illegitimate. The efforts of the Massachusetts Prince Hall Grand Lodge to regain its warrant, or to get recognition from the United Grand Lodge of England proved fruitless. So from 1824 on, all black Masonic lodges were considered "clandestine,"— illegal, or not really Masonic—by white Freemasons. For over two hundred years all state Grand Lodges had black counterparts. It was an alternate Masonic universe.

Beginning in 1989, U.S. Grand Lodges slowly began to recognize their Prince Hall counterparts. This involved a formal acceptance of Prince Hall lodges as legitimate, and extension of the right of mutual visitation to each other's members.

What speeded the movement was the acceptance of the Prince Hall Grand Lodge of Massachusetts by the United Grand Lodge of England in 1994. The English Grand Lodge did not admit any mistakes in canceling the original 1784 warrant, but it did extend recognition. This "healing" of the warrant removed any legitimate reason by

American Grand Lodges for withholding Masonic recognition from Prince Hall Masons.

Beginning in 1995, Grand Lodges all over the United States began to recognize Prince Hall Masonry. Despite some racial ugliness, the movement swept through the country and made steady progress. As of 2026, just two U.S. Grand Lodges still have shamefully refused to accept the obvious, and recognize black Freemasonry in some form. They are the Grand Lodges of South Carolina, and Mississippi. West Virginia and Louisiana have acknowledged Prince Hall Masonry in another state, but not in their own. This at least shows *some* recognition of realities. Until these last stubborn Grand Lodges come to their senses, they will continue to provide evidence that critics can use to smear Freemasonry with the charge of racism.*

"I bet you if I met him and had a chat with him, I'd find him a very interesting and human fellow because, you know, I really never met a man that I didn't like."

     ---Brother Will Rogers, Claremore Lodge No. 53, Oklahoma.

Fellowship

The symbol of the so-called "Knife and Fork Degree." Not a serious Masonic emblem. It is obviously derived from the traditional Square and Compasses. This humorous Masonic symbol stems from the traditional feeling that many Freemasons seem to be more concerned with the food and drink served after the Stated Meeting than with anything else. As with most Masonic subjects, there is a serious element to this discussion. The Fraternity is, ultimately, about spreading the ties of Brotherhood amongst its membership. From earliest times, the meal after the meeting was an integral part of this process. Accordingly, in North American lodges this tradition has been continued. It can consist of anything from a casual snack of sandwiches and coffee to a sit-down dinner complete with appetizers and a dessert. In many European lodges, a formal dinner is held, complete with alcoholic beverages and extensive toasts.

Come, let us prepare,
We Brothers that are
Assembled on merry occasion;
Let's drink, laugh and sing.
Our wine has a spring,
Here's Health to an Accepted Mason!

—Old Masonic drinking song
Mathew Birkhead, 1722*

ULTIMATE PURPOSES

We have tried to cover as much ground as possible in this short little book. The psychology, origins, and historical development of Freemasonry have been explored. The ritual of a generic meeting, along with the degree system, have been outlined. Some of the challenges, problems, and dangers to the Fraternity have been revealed. The overall structure of the movement, with its various options and permutations, has been demystified (I hope).

Is there anything left to talk about? Has any facet of Masonry been neglected? I think there is one, last, obvious question to be addressed. Why? Why do men around the world participate in this group with its strange rituals, customs, and idealistic goals? What possible rewards can there be for the individual? Friends, family, and co-workers, have often ended conversations with these questions. My general answer is that Freemasonry has a wide variety of benefits to offer, although these advantages are subtle, and depend on the individual.

First, and most obviously, Freemasonry offers a new arena for achievement and advancement. The new member sees an organization that is entirely dependent on each man volunteering his time and efforts. There are no paid positions, and leadership changes each year. There is a continual need for "new blood" if the Fraternity is to stay healthy. Each candidate is honestly needed by his lodge to contribute his talents and potential.

If a brand-new Brother works hard, and learns the customs and ritual of the group, he can look forward to becoming Worshipful Master of his lodge in just a few years. In the Appendant orders, the situation is much the same. New officers are always in demand.

The mechanics of learning to become a Masonic

leader are also valuable. In order to play an active role in one's lodge, public speaking is a must. The process of becoming an officer involves an extensive course in learning to communicate with groups, and efficiently run a large meeting. These are skills that are transferable to many other walks of life.

Next, this leadership training partly consists of learning to harness the human memory. This is a lost skill in the modern world. Before the advent of printing, humans routinely had to memorize vast amounts of information. This ability has been largely lost. Only a few professions like politics or the theater, require a good memory. Masonry reawakens this amazing human ability.

Finally, politics and religion are forbidden subjects within a Masonic lodge. Members are forced to interact with each other minus the cues of class, wealth, political opinion, or religious belief. Freemasons address each other as "Brother." With the aid of this artificial, formal method of socializing, Freemasons are able to achieve deep, honest, long lasting bonds of friendship and respect. If these were the only advantages to membership, they would make a formidable case for becoming a Freemason.

There are problems, of course. No group is perfect. Like any human institution, the Craft sometimes appears to stray from its ideals. Many men join the Fraternity, and after a few months or years, decide that it is little more than a glorified men's club, with an empty set of meaningless rituals. It *can* become tedious if members fail to fully embrace those ideals, or lose sight of their purpose.

The defining aspect of Freemasonry is the shared, initiative experience. Although most social groups have a rite of membership, the Brotherhood is unique in this respect. Joining most institutions is a one-time experience. After becoming a member, individuals resume their individual lives and perspectives. What remains is a pleasant memory.

Freemasonry is different, however. The ultimate purpose of a Lodge is to reenact the entrance ceremony over and over again. It is obviously important for the new member, but repetition enables the Freemason to continuously explore anew the experience. Layers of meaning are added while the individual becomes ever more entwined with the Brotherhood.

With repetition comes mastery of the ritual and deeper ties with one's fellows. This can alleviate some of the pressures of existence. Modern life can become a battle for one's sanity. All day, every day, forces compete for our attention and energy. Family, children, job, taxes, wife, in-laws, parents, friends, politics, the list seems endless—and relentless. Sometimes it's hard to find a small space for oneself to breath. Freemasonry can give one that space.

Ceremony is as old as human civilization and has many purposes. It can commemorate the dead, celebrate good luck, mark the seasons, or get us in touch with our higher purposes. Masonic ritual addresses all of these different aspects of human aspiration.

The lodge provides a quiet place where one can meet real friends who simply wish the pleasure of each others company. Ritual can have a transforming effect on oneself, and on others. By taking on a role, or a different persona, during the ceremony, we become "other." We lose ourselves in something larger. Masonic ritual gives its participants a vision of the good, the true, and the beautiful that remains in the soul even after returning to the chaos and confusion of everyday life.

During the ceremony, something happens within the individual. By submitting to the unique details of ritual, we give ourselves up to a larger pattern and create—at least for that short instance—a unity of time, space, heaven, earth, and of the eternal in all of us.*

It is this aspect of Freemasonry that is the most valuable part of membership. The other, tangible benefits are wonderful, but they pale in comparison to these opportunities for true inner peace and fellowship. Within this safe, welcoming atmosphere, every man is free to develop himself in harmony with his fellows. I think Brother Francois Marie Arouet expressed it best. He was sponsored by Brother Benjamin Franklin, and initiated into the Lodge of the Nine Sisters in Paris, 1778. He is better known by his pen name, Voltaire. In one of his novels, he has a character repeat this advice over and over: "We must cultivate our garden."* This is what Freemasonry gives each member: the space, time, and peace to cultivate one's spirit and become a better man.

END NOTES

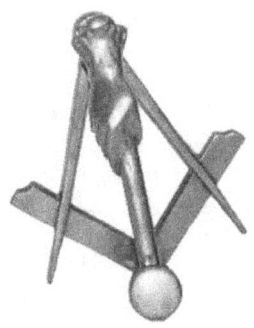

  *Masonic door knocker. This is a common piece of decoration in most lodges. Usually it is installed on the door that separates the Preparing Room from the Lodge Room proper. When new candidates are ready to receive the Masonic degrees they are directed to place their hands on it and knock three times on the door. In most jurisdictions the supplicant is blindfolded and must rely on his Guide in order to find the door. This part of the ceremony symbolizes man's groping toward knowledge and enlightenment. The three knocks are taken from Mathew 7: 7-8, "Ask and it will be given to you; seek and you will find; knock and the door will be opened to you."**

Chapter 1 "Tile"

Page 11—*Tile*... Henry Wilson Coil, *Coil's Masonic Encyclopedia* (Richmond: Macoy Publishing, 1995), 653.

Page 14—*Listed in the National Register*... Waldman, Glenys A. and Michael R. Harrison. *The Masonic Temple in Philadelphia: A National Historic Landmark* (Philadelphia, PA: The Masonic Library and Museum of Pennsylvania, 2013), 1.

Page 16—*The Great Secret of Freemasonry*... This is possibly apocryphal. From the Grand Lodge of Massachusetts website: http://www.massfreemasonry.org/index.tpl?ng_view=19

Page 17—*The All-Seeing Eye*...*Coil's Masonic Encyclopedia, 27.* Verse from Proverbs 15:3, *New American Bible, St. Joseph Edition* (New York: Catholic Book Publishing Co., 1992).

Chapter 2 "Opening"

Page 19—*Opening*...*Coil's Masonic Encyclopedia,* 457.

Page 20—*John Wayne*...Harold V.B. Voorhis, *Facts for Freemasons,* (Richmond, VA: Macoy Publishing Co.:1979). 124-69.

Page 22—*society*...Roger Scruton, *A Dictionary of Political Thought* (New York: Hill and Wang, 1984). 149.

Page 22—*Grande dames*...Leading ladies of the time, usually of noble birth and wealth, who had the leisure to cultivate the leading minds of the day and sponsor writers and intellectuals through patronage.

Page 23—*social order*...Margaret C. Jacob, *Living the Enlightenment: Freemasonry and Politics in Eighteenth-Century Europe* (Oxford: Oxford University Press, 1991), 3.

Page 25—*Early Ceremony*...picture taken by the author from his private collection.

Page 27—*always problematical*...Louis I. Bredvold & Ralph Gl Ross, eds. *The Philosophy of Edmund Burke* (Ann Arbor: University of Michigan Press, 1970), 35.

Page 27—*or anyone else*...George Lakoff *The Political Mind: Why You Can't Understand 21st Century Politics with an 18th Century Brain* (New York: Viking, 2008), 7-9.

Chapter 3 "Greeting"

Page 29—*you dear brother*...*Coil's Masonic Encyclopedia,* 306.

Page 30—"Father is Brother After Son Confers Degree," The Pennsylvania Freemason Vol. XLIX, November 2002, No. 4.

Page 31—*histories of Freemasonry begin*...Henry Wilson Coil, *A Comprehensive View of Freemasonry* (Richmond, VA: Macoy Publishing & Supply Co., 1998), 69-71.

Page 32—*to the Crusades*...Two modern authors that embrace this theory are John J. Robinson *Born in Blood: The Lost Secrets of Freemasonry* (New York: M. Evans & Company, 1989), and Michael Baigent and Henry Leigh *The Temple and the Lodge* (New York: Arcade Publishing, 1989). Since Freemasonry first made its appearance in the United Kingdom, both books theorize that, after the suppression of the Order of the Templars in 1307, refugees made their way to England and set up a clandestine, secret organization to ensure the protection of surviving members. Much like the Nazi ODESSA, they laid low until better times, waiting to reemerge from the darkness.

Page 33—*to be crushed*...Thomas S. Kuhn, *The Structure of Scientific Revolutions*, (Chicago, IL: The University of Chicago Press, 1970). This book explores some of the problems when new scientific theories are advanced in a culture.

Page 35—*in this affair*...Alan Cowell, "After 350 Years, Vatican Says Galileo was Right: It Moves," *The New York Times*, October 31, 1992, A-1.

Page 35—*into gold*... Francis A. Yates, *The Rosicrucian Enlightenment,* New York, NY: Routledge, 1972, 204-05.

Page 36—*from 1583 to 1585*... Francis A. Yates, *The Art of Memory*, (Chicago, IL: The University of Chicago Press, 1966), 199-204.

Page 37—*works in Scotland.* Coil, *A Comprehensive View of Freemasonry*, 54.

Page 37—*of Masonic Lodges*...Coil, *A Comprehensive View of Freemasonry,* 54.

Page 37—*ancient era of the Romans and Greeks.* For example, see Jasper Ridley, *The Freemasons: A History of the World's Most Powerful Secret Society* (New York: Arcade Publishing, 2001), 1-8.

Page 38—*During the "Dark Ages!"*...Lionel Vibert, "Anderson's Constitutions of 1723" in *Little Masonic Library, Volume 1* (Richmond, VA: Macoy Publishing & Supply Co., 1977), 169-71.

Page 39—*"republican" activities*... Margaret C. Jacob, *Living the Enlightenment: Freemasonry and Politics in Eighteenth-Century Europe* (Oxford: Oxford University Press, 1991). 3-8.

Page 40—*within his kingdom*... Maynard Solomon, *Mozart: A Life* (New York: HarperCollins Publishers, 1995). 321-335.

Page 40—*the mid-1800's...* Alfonso Scirocco, *Garibaldi, Citizen of the World: A Biography* (Princeton, NJ: Princeton University Press, 2007) 33, 121, 381-82.

Page 40—*has been suppressed...* Jasper Ridley, *The Freemasons: A History of the World's Most Powerful Secret Society* (New York: Arcade Publishing, 2001) 236-56.

Page 41—*the year 1959...* Masonic Service Association of North America. "Membership Totals since 1924." MSA. Web, 2008. http://www.msana.com/msastats.asp.

Chapter 4 "Minutes"

Page 47—*Fatherhood of God...*Common Masonic saying.

Page 49—*within London society...* Coil, *A Comprehensive View of Freemasonry*, 69-70.

Page 50—*for oblivion...* Coil, *A Comprehensive View...*, 72-81.

Page 51—*of Scotland in 1736...*Christopher Hodapp, *Freemasons for Dummies,* (Hoboken, NJ: John Wiley & Sons, 2013),34.

Page 52—*the fledgling national government...*This is a very hard proposition to prove beyond a reasonable historical doubt. The researcher is left with seeing much Masonic "smoke" in this period, but no hard, written documentation proving that there was any "fire." What has been proven is that many revolutionary leaders were members of *both* the Sons of Liberty and the Freemasons—especially in Boston. See Allen E. Roberts, *Freemasonry in American History*, (Richmond, VA: Macoy Publishing Co. Inc., 1985), Chapter 15, pp. 146-161. For an in depth analysis of the Masonic structures within Washington's army I recommend Steven C. Bullock, *Revolutionary Brotherhood: Freemasonry and the Transformation of* *the American Social Order, 1730-1840,* (Chapel Hill, NC: University of North Carolina Press, 1996), especially Chapter 4, 121-133.

Page 53—*anti-masonry*...See Bullock,277-278.

Page 54—*other political movements*... Many members, along with Temperance and anti-slavery activists, Know Nothing's, and Whigs, eventually found a home in the Republican Party. See Bullock, 291-293.

Page 55—*United States.* U.S. Department of Commerce, U.S. Census Bureau. "Demographic Trends in the 20th Century: Census 2000 Special Reports." Appendix A, Table 1. "Total Population for the United States, Regions, and States: 1900 to 2000." U.S. Census Bureau, 2002. Web. www.census.gov/prod/2002pubs/censr-4.pdf. Masonic Service Association of North America. "Membership Totals since 1924." MSA. Web, 2021. http://www.msana.com/msastats.asp.

Chapter 5 "Communications"

Page 60—*used in the ritual.* Descriptions of the building of Solomon's Temple can be found in 1 Kings Chapters 6-8. *The Holy Bible, KJV*, Wichita: Heirloom Bible Pub, 1988.

Chapter 6 "Business"

Page 80—*feelings of embarrassment...* For a good exploration of the feelings and emotions felt during the ceremony, I recommend Leo Tolstoy's *War and Peace*, Signet Classics, (The New American Library, New York: 1968),426-41. In writing about Pierre Bezukhov's initiation, Tolstoy captures perfectly the awkwardness, the fear, and the awe that a candidate feels when taking this first Masonic step.

Page 81—*the Entered Apprentice Degree*...In the craft guilds, the first step in the process of becoming a skilled craftsman was to be enrolled as an apprentice to a master workman. After a period of years, as the apprentice gained skill and experience, he would be advanced within his craft guild. See *Coil's Masonic Encyclopedia,* 63.

Page 83—*"profane" world*...This term simply refers to those outside the Fraternity. It is an example of a general term in the English language used in a specific, purely Masonic way. There are many such examples of this phenomenon in Masonry.

Page 84—*his promise*... I've always found it interesting that George Washington, on taking the Oath of office on April 30, 1789 incorporated this gesture into the ceremony. Harry Truman, upon taking the oath for the first time in 1945, also kissed the Holy Bible. Both men had served as Worshipful Masters. James Thomas Flexner, *George Washington and the New Nation (1783-1793)*, (New York: Little, Brown and Company, 1969). 187. Also, see David McCullough, *Truman*, (New York: Simon & Schuster, 1992), p. 347.

Page 85—*solemn oaths taken*... *Holy Bible, KJV*, Wichita: Heirloom Bible Pub, 1988. Ruth 4:7.

Page 85—*the conferring officer*... The brother who recites the Degree and runs the ceremony is temporarily the Worshipful Master of the lodge during the ritual. He wears all the garb and accoutrements of the office. After the Degree is completed, he is relieved by the actual, serving, Worshipful Master.

Page 92—*and astronomy*...Henry W. Coil, *Coil's Masonic Encyclopedia,* (Richmond, VA: Macoy Publishing & Masonic Supply Co. Inc., 1995), 378.

Page 92—*happy and fulfilled life...* H.L. Haywood, *The Great Teachings of Masonry,* (Richmond, VA: Macoy Publishing & Supply Co. Inc., 1986), 141-42.

Page 95—*individual life plan...* Allen E. Roberts, *The Craft and Its Symbols: Opening the Door to Masonic Symbolism,* (Richmond, VA: Macoy Publishing Company, Inc., 1974), 51-52.

Page 99—*in his presence...Holy Bible, KJV*, Wichita: Heirloom Bible Pub, 1988. Exodus 3:2-6.

Page 100—*Constitutions of the Freemasons...* Facsimile reprint in *The Little Masonic Library, Book I,* (Richmond, VA: Macoy Publishing & Supply Co., Inc., 1977), 159-274.

Page 100—*within the ritual...* Since Masonic secrecy has always been a priority, it is almost impossible to trace the development of the ritual during this period. Such clues as we have are due to the existence of Masonic "exposés," in which critics of the fraternity published pirated versions of the ritual. One of the earliest of these works was anonymously published in Dublin, Ireland in 1777. Entitled *M*h*b**e, or The Grand Lodge Door Open'd*, it has been republished in facsimile form. (Kessinger Publishing Company, Kila, MT, 2006).

Page 100—*Hiram Abiff...* No satisfactory translation of the surname "Abiff" has been discovered. Some biblical scholars feel that it can be taken to mean "the widow's son," some editions of the Bible simply include it as a meaningless name or title.

Chapter 7 "Reports"

Page 115—*New York City...The Shrine* (Pittsburgh, PA: Hiller Publishing Co., 1977), 17.

Page 115—*philanthropy...,* Ibid, 207.

Chapter 8 "Closing"

Page 117—www.themasonictrowel.com/clipart/Blue
_Lodge/blue_page_29.htm

Page 119—*Freed Masons...*Wayne A. Huss *The Master Builders:
A History of the Grand Lodge of Free and Accepted Masons of
Pennsylvania, 3 Volumes,* (Philadelphia, PA: Grand Lodge, F. &
A.M. of Pennsylvania, 1986), Vol. I, 4.

Page 120—*for joining...* Robert C. Broderick, Ed. *The Catholic
Encyclopedia,* (New York: Thomas Nelson Pub., 1987), 229.

Page 120—*freedom of conscience...*John J. Robinson, *Born in
Blood: The Lost Secrets of Freemasonry,* (New York: M. Evans &
Co.: 1989), 345-59. This work contains a fair translation of the
Latin document. The official Vatican version is wordier, but the
meaning is the same.

Page 121—*against the Church...*Robert C. Broderick, Ed. 375.

Page 121—*culture to another...* *Catechism of the Catholic
Church,* (The Vatican: 1994), 466.

Page 124—*pure fabrication...*Henry Wilson Coil, *Masonic
Encyclopedia,* 647.

Page 124—*case unsolved...*John J. Robinson, 305.

Page 124—*with it as well...*John J. Robinson, 313-317.

Page 127—*charge of racism...*Henry Wilson Coil, *Masonic
Encyclopedia,* 99-101. Also updated 2/4/26.
freemasonsfordummies.blogspot, updated 2/4/2026.

Chapter 9 "Fellowship"

Page130—www.masonic-poetry.org/poems/entapsng.htm Date: 22/06/2006.

Page 134—*all of us...* Karen Armstrong, *The Great Transformation: The Beginning of our Religious Traditions*, (New York: Alfred A. Knopf. 2006), 76.

Page 134—*our garden...* Voltaire, *Candide*, (New York: Bantam Books, 1971), 120.

End Notes

Page 137—*Ask...*from *New American Bible, St. Joseph Ed.* (New York: Catholic Book Publishing Company, 1992).

Bibliography

Page 145—*Beehive...*from *Coil's Masonic Encyclopedia,* 90.

Bibliography

*The Beehive. A good symbol for the bibliographic
section of a book. A Masonic element that dates from at least the
early Nineteenth Century. An early Masters lecture says that it—
and the bees that are associated with it "...is an emblem of
industry, and recommends the practice of that virtue to all created
beings...It teaches us, that as we come into the world rational and
intelligent beings, so we should ever be industrious ones; never
sitting down contented while our fellow-creatures around us are
in want, especially when it is in our power to relieve them, without
inconvenience to ourselves."**

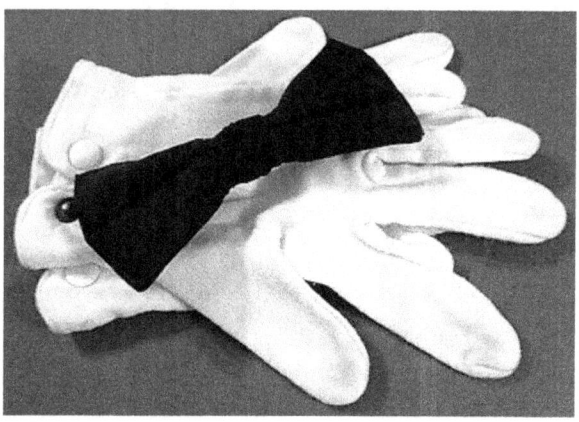

Black bow-tie and white gloves. Part of the wardrobe of many
well-dressed Freemasons. The tie is part of formal dress.
The white gloves reminds the Mason that his hands—and heart—should
be pure at all times.

Armstrong, Karen. *The Great Transformation: The Beginning of Our Religious Traditions*, New York: Alfred A. Knopf, 2006.

Broderick, Ed., Robert C. *The Catholic Encyclopedia*, New York: Thomas Nelson Publishers, 1987.

Bredvold, Louis I. and Ralph G. Ross. *The Philosophy of Edmund Burke,* Ann Arbor: University of Michigan Press, 1970.

Bullock, Steven C. *Revolutionary Brotherhood: Freemasonry and the and the Transformation of the American Social Order, 1730-1840,* Chapel Hill, NC: University of North Carolina Press, 1996.

Burtt, Robert E. *A Pennsylvania Masonic Handbook*, North Charlestown, SC: Createspace, 2010.

Catechism of the Catholic Church, The Vatican: 1994.

Coil, Henry Wilson, *A Comprehensive View of Freemasonry,* Richmond, VA: Macoy Publishing & Masonic Supply Co., Inc., 1998.

--------------. *Outlines of Freemasonry,* Kessinger Publishing Co. LLC, Kila, MT, 2008.

--------------. *Coil's Masonic Encyclopedia,* Richmond, VA: Macoy Publishing & Masonic Supply Co. Inc., 1995.

Davis, Robert G. *The Mason's Words: The History and Evolution of the American Masonic Ritual,* Guthrie, OK: Building Stone Publishing, 2013.

Flexner, James Thomas. *George Washington and the New Nation (1783-1793)*, New York: Little, Brown and Company, 1969.

Gorley, Shawn M. *Freemasonry Defined: Using History to Understand the Fraternity,* Raleigh, NC: Lulu, 2013.

Haywood, H.L. *The Great Teachings of Masonry,* Richmond, VA: Macoy Publishing & Supply Co. Inc., 1986.

Hodapp, Christopher, *Freemasons for Dummies,* Hoboken, NJ: John Wiley & Sons, Inc.: 2013.

The Holy Bible, KJV, Wichita: Heirloom Bible Pub, 1988.

Huss, Wayne A. *The Master Builders: A History of the Grand Lodge of Free and Accepted Masons of Pennsylvania, 3 Volumes,* Philadelphia, PA: Grand Lodge, F. & A.M. of Pennsylvania, 1986.

Jacob, Margaret C. *Living the Enlightenment: Freemasonry and Politics in Eighteenth-Century Europe*, Oxford: Oxford University Press, 1991.

Kuhn, Thomas S., *The Structure of Scientific Revolutions*, Chicago, IL: The University of Chicago Press, 1970.

Lakoff, George. *The Political Mind.* New York: Viking, 2008.

The Little Masonic Library, 5 Volumes. Richmond, VA: Macoy Publishing & Supply Co., Inc., 1977.

M*h*b**e, or The Grand Lodge Door Open'd, facsimile edition, Kila, MT: Kessinger Publishing Company, 2006.

McCullough, David. *Truman*, New York: Simon & Schuster, 1992.

The New American Bible, Saint Joseph Edition. New York: Catholic Book Publishing Company, 1992.

Pirsig, Robert M. *Zen and the Art of Motorcycle Maintenance: An Inquiry into Values,* New York: Bantam Books, 1976.

Ridley, Jasper. *The Freemasons: A History of the World's Most Powerful Secret Society,* New York: Arcade Pub., 2001.

Roberts, Allen E., *The Craft and Its Symbols: Opening the Door to Masonic Symbolism,* Richmond, VA: Macoy Publishing and Masonic Supply Company, Inc., 1974.

----------------. *Freemasonry in American History*, Richmond, VA: Macoy Publishing & Masonic Supply Co. Inc., 1985.

Robinson, John J. *Born in Blood: The Lost Secrets of Freemasonry,* New York: M. Evans & Co.: 1989.

Scirocco, Alfonso. *Garibaldi, Citizen of the World: A Biography,* Princeton, NJ: Princeton University Press, 2007.

Scruton, Roger. *A Dictionary of Political Thought,* New York: Hill and Wang, 1984.

The Shrine, Pittsburgh, PA: Hiller Publishing Co., 1977.

Solomon, Maynard. *Mozart: A Life,* New York: HarperCollins Publishers, 1995.

Stevenson, David. *The Origins of Freemasonry,* Cambridge: Cambridge University Press, 1998.

Tolstoy, Leo. *War and Peace*, New Library, New York: 1968.

Voltaire, *Candide*, New York: Bantam Books, 1971.

Voorhis, Harold V.B. *Facts for Freemason*, Richmond, VA:

Macoy Publishing and Supply Co., 1977.

Waldman, Glenys A. and Michael R. Harrison. *The Masonic Temple in Philadelphia: A National Historic Landmark,* Philadelphia, PA: The Masonic Library and Museum of Pennsylvania, 2013.

Yates, Francis A. *The Rosicrucian Enlightenment,* New York, NY: Routledge, 1972.

--------------------. *The Art of Memory*, Chicago, IL: The University of Chicago Press, 1966.

INTERNET RESOURCES

massfreemasonry.org/index.tpl?ng_view=19

census.gov/prod/2002pubs/censr-4.pdf

msana.com/msastats.asp

bessel.org/masrec/phamap.htm

brainyquote.com/quotes/authors

Note: all illustrations not attributed, were drawn, photographed or otherwise privately produced by the author.

Brother George Washington as Master of his Lodge, 1794.
Uniquely, Washington was elected Worshipful Master of
Alexandria Lodge No. 22 while also serving as
President of the United States.

About the Author

The author's Masonic ring. Freemasons are proud of their organization and usually sport jewelry, pins, or other personal items that advertise their affiliation. A ring is probably the most common article. It serves two purposes. First, it signals other Brethren of one's status in the Fraternity. Second, it serves as a subtle way to "spread the word" about Freemasonry to the general public (the profane). Until recently, advertising by most Grand Lodges was not done. The only way to attract new members was through personal interaction. Rings and pins helped to establish a public presence in the community by members.

Even today, wearing a ring is a good way to meet Brethren and form new bonds. I have met many fellow Masons in airports, stores, and public events who noticed my ring and started a conversation based on our common, shared bond.

*"Live in such a way that you would not be ashamed
to sell your parrot to the town gossip."*

*--Brother Will Rogers
Claremore Lodge No. 53, Oklahoma*

Robert E. Burtt was born in Du Bois, Pennsylvania in 1954. An alumnus of the University of Pittsburgh, he earned B.A., M.A. and M.P.A degrees there. He is also a veteran of the U.S. Navy. He currently earns his bread as a minor functionary within the U.S. Department of Homeland Security.

He was raised a Master Mason in Harmony Lodge No. 429, Zelienople, PA in 1995. He is a Past Master of Harmony Lodge. A member of Delta Royal Arch Chapter No. 170, New Castle, PA, he is Past High Priest. He also belongs to Hiram Council No. 45, Royal and Select Master Masons where he is Past Thrice Illustrious Master. He was knighted in Lawrence Commandary No. 62, and is Past Eminent Commander.

Brother Burtt is a Charter Member of the Pennsylvania Lodge of Research.

He was also awarded the title Master Masonic Scholar by the Grand Lodge of Pennsylvania's Academy of Masonic Knowledge in 2021.

Mr. Burtt is married to the love of his life, Grace, and lives in Little Rock, Arkansas. Without her encouragement and support, his writing career would not have been possible.

"Secrecy is the element in all Goodness;
Even Virtue, even Beauty, is Mysterious."

--Thomas Carlyle